# Right Fielders Are People Too

## An Inclusive Approach to Teaching Middle School Physical Education

### JOHN HICHWA

Illustrated by
**PEDRO LEITÃO**

**Human Kinetics**

Library of Congress Cataloging-in-Publication Data

Hichwa, John, 1938–
    Right fielders are people too : an inclusive approach to teaching middle school physical education / John Hichwa
        p.  cm.
    ISBN 0-88011-856-3
    1. Physical education and training--Study and teaching (Middle school)--United States   I. Title.
    GV223.H52  1998
    613.7'0712--dc21                                                                97-40896
                                                                                    CIP

ISBN: 0-88011-856-3

**Acquisitions Editor:** Scott Wikgren; **Managing Editor:** Coree Schutter; **Assistant Editor:** Erin Sprague; **Copyeditor:** Cinci Stowell; **Proofreader:** Alesha Thompson; **Graphic Designer:** Nancy Rasmus; **Graphic Artist:** Doug Burnett; **Cover Designer:** Jack Davis; **Illustrator (interior and cover):** Pedro Leitão; **Printer:** United Graphics

Printed in the United States of America

10 9 8 7 6 5 4 3 2 1

**Human Kinetics**
Web site: http://www.humankinetics.com/

*United States:* Human Kinetics, P.O. Box 5076, Champaign, IL 61825-5076
1-800-747-4457
e-mail: humank@hkusa.com

*Canada:* Human Kinetics, Box 24040, Windsor, ON N8Y 4Y9
1-800-465-7301 (in Canada only)
e-mail: humank@hkcanada.com

*Europe:* Human Kinetics, P.O. Box IW14, Leeds LS16 6TR, United Kingdom
(44) 1132 781708
e-mail: humank@hkeurope.com

*Australia:* Human Kinetics, 57A Price Avenue, Lower Mitcham, South Australia 5062
(088) 277 1555
e-mail: humank@hkaustralia.com

*New Zealand:* Human Kinetics, P.O. Box 105-231, Auckland 1
(09) 523 3462
e-mail: humank@hknewz.com

For Marion, P.W.M.
(Perfect wife and mother)
Master teacher of young children.

I thank you for all your help in writing this book.

I love you,
John

# Lineup

## A Double Header

### Play Ball: Game #1

## Play Ball: Game #2

# Extra Innings

# Acknowledgments

I have been blessed in many ways.

First and foremost, Marion, my wife, has been my inspiration, critic, ghost writer, and partner for over 38 years. She exudes a presence of confidence, creativity, and a marvelous work ethic. With her prodding and enthusiastic support, I have prepared this document as a testament of our years of working with children. I have faith and confidence in today's teachers and students, and I hope that this offering in some small way will help guide both students and teachers to become productive, responsible, active, and caring members of society.

My all-time favorite students are Michael, Diane, and Jill, our children. Their unsolicited, honest, and constructive comments helped me better understand the feelings and needs of all my students. They continue to help me with my writings and provide suggestions to improve my presentations. Their own lives continue to be an inspiration to me.

Karl Rohnke, one of the originators of Project Adventure, has been my mentor and friend for over 20 years. His creativity, insights, and writings continue to guide my own thinking on how to best work with students and teachers. Karl, without a doubt, has been the one teacher who has had the most influence on me and my work. I am indebted to him.

For 35 years, I had the privilege of working with students, parents, colleagues, and administrators in the Redding, CT, school system. The school, gymnasiums, and outdoor facilities were my laboratories, where I experimented and developed my teaching style. I was fortunate to have support and encouragement to try new things. Nancy Bowen, my physical education colleague at the John Read Middle School for 13 years, deserves a special plaudit. We bounced ideas off each other and planned together. I thank her for her enthusiasm, encouragement, professional advice, and the fun we had together.

I am indebted to Pedro Leitão, of Nove Oeiras, Portugal, for his masterful artwork. His illustrations make the manuscript come alive. I appreciate his artistic talent and all the time and effort he so willingly gave.

J.S.H.
Redding, CT

# About the Title

"Right Field" is a song written by Willy Welch and recorded by Peter, Paul, and Mary on the Gold Castle Records label. It appeared on the album entitled "No Easy Walk to Freedom." The song is about a youngster who is not a very good athlete and is always chosen last.

Willy Welch also wrote a book entitled *Playing Right Field*. It is illustrated by Marc Simont and published by Scholastic, Inc., New York, NY.

The first time I heard the song, I thought of some of my students who lacked the self-confidence, skill, or both to feel comfortable getting in and playing the game, but wanted to. I titled this book *Right Fielders Are People Too*, because I feel so strongly about the importance of physical education teachers providing the environment and challenges that allow all students to work to their potential. Students need the opportunity to learn skills without intimidation and to experience the joy and exhilaration of physical activities, even if they cannot perform the activities so very well.

# "Right Field"

written by Willy Welch
(c) 1986 Playing Right Music (ASCAP) 3:36

Saturday summers—when I was a kid,
We'd run to the school yard and here's what we did.
We'd pick out the captains and choose up the teams.
It was always the measure of my self-esteem,
Because the strongest and fastest played shortstop and first.
Last ones they picked were the worst.
I never needed to ask. It was sealed
I just took up my place in RIGHT FIELD.

PLAYING RIGHT FIELD, IT'S EASY YOU KNOW.
YOU CAN BE AWKWARD AND YOU CAN BE SLOW.
THAT'S WHY I'M HERE IN RIGHT FIELD,
WATCHING THE DANDELIONS GROW.

Playing RIGHT FIELD can be lonely and dull.

Little Leagues never have lefties that pull.

I dream of the day they hit one my way.

They never did. But still I would pray

That I make a fantastic catch on the run

And not lose the ball in the sun.

Then I'd awake from this long reverie

And pray that the ball never came out to me.

HERE IN RIGHT FIELD, IT'S EASY YOU KNOW.

YOU CAN BE AWKWARD AND YOU CAN BE SLOW.

THAT'S WHY I'M HERE IN RIGHT FIELD,

WATCHING THE DANDELIONS GROW.

Off in the distance the game's dragging on.

There are strikes on the batter; some runners are on.

I don't know the inning. I've forgotten the score.

The whole team is yelling and I don't know what for.

Suddenly everyone's looking at me.

My mind has been wondering. What could it be?

They point to the sky and I look up above.

And a baseball . . . falls . . . into . . . my . . . glove!

HERE IN RIGHT FIELD, IT'S IMPORTANT YOU KNOW.

YOU'VE GOT TO KNOW HOW TO CATCH. YOU'VE GOT TO

KNOW HOW TO THROW.

THAT'S WHY I'M HERE IN RIGHT FIELD,

WATCHING THE DANDELIONS GROW.

# Debriefing "Right Field"

After listening to the recording or reading the words of the song "Right Field," think about and discuss what messages it conveys. Do the words focus your thoughts on the often-forgotten feelings individual children may have?

Debrief with your students or colleagues by asking questions such as the following:

- What issues are brought out in the song?
- Do you personally relate to this song in any way?
- How would you feel about your class if you were a "right fielder"?
- What changes could we make so that all students feel good about themselves and others?
- What do you see as the main objective of sports in a physical education class?
- In what ways could teams be chosen so that all students feel comfortable and valued?
- How can we help make "right fielders" enjoy physical activities for a lifetime?
- Do you think a young "right fielder" has any possibility of becoming a good athlete when older?
- In the song, the right fielder becomes a hero. How often does that happen in real life?

My hope is to have every child grow up without being able to relate to this song. This book is written to help teachers dream big, plan well, and make every child a winner.

# Let the Games Begin

*Right Fielders Are People Too* is divided into two sections or games. The first game gives an overview of various characteristics of the middle school child and describes an effective middle school physical education program. The second section, Game #2, has specific suggestions for planning the day-to-day activities.

## Content Standards in Physical Education

The National Association for Sport and Physical Education established content standards for school physical education programs that clearly identify statements related to what a student should know and be able to do as a result of a quality physical education program. A list of the content standards which apply to the concepts and activities of each inning are listed at the beginning of the 3rd-7th Innings in Game #1 and in all the innings in Game #2.

I highly recommend that you contact NASPE and purchase the entire document entitled *Moving Into the Future—National Standards for Physical Education: A Guide to Content and Assessment.*

This document states the following.

# A physically educated student:

1. Demonstrates competency in many movement forms and proficiency in a few movement forms.
2. Applies movement concepts and principles to the learning and development of motor skills.
3. Exhibits a physically active lifestyle.
4. Achieves and maintains a health-enhancing level of physical fitness.
5. Demonstrates responsible personal and social behavior in physical-activity settings.
6. Demonstrates understanding and respect for differences among people in physical-activity settings.
7. Understands that physical activity provides opportunities for enjoyment, challenge, self-expression, and social interaction.

Reprinted from *Moving Into the Future: National Standards for Physical Educationt* (1995) with permission from the National Association for Sport and Physical Education (NASPE), 1900 Association Drive, Reston, VA 20191-1599.

# PLAY BALL

# GAME #1

**Developing an inclusive physical education program for the middle school student**

# 1st Inning

# To Know Them Is to Love Them

"High school is going great, but I really miss my physical education classes. We became so close. I'll have good and bad teachers as I go through high school, but I will always remember you as not only my gym teacher, but also as one who helped us through some really tough years."

—Ninth grade student

Most students beginning their middle school education are entering puberty. They will experience more important changes during this period of their lives than at any other time except their first year of life. They will change physically, mentally, emotionally, sexually, and socially. This period of rapid growth marks the end of childhood and the start of physical and sexual maturity.

Because of the many changes taking place in a relatively short time, middle school students often experience many conflicts and frustrations. Their social, physical, and emotional problems often intertwine. Their physical development often plays a role in their social and emotional behavior.

How middle school students see themselves—adult or childlike, attractive or unattractive, smart or stupid, athletic or clumsy, popular or unpopular—partially determines their behavior. Unfortunately, student self-perception at this age is often not very accurate and the self-concept is likely to sink to an all-time low. Any perceived shortcoming may be exaggerated in the student's mind and cause much anguish. The significance of body development, physical features, hairstyles, clothes, and the importance of friends are also often exaggerated. A pimple may make a student feel socially unacceptable. The environment has a great influence on student behavior and self-esteem. An inclusive and developmentally appropriate physical education curriculum is essential for students to feel comfortable in class and developing a positive attitude toward physical activities.

As a result of physical growth, interests and needs also change among middle school youngsters. These changes have a considerable influence on their social development, and students begin to take a strong interest in the opposite sex. The strangeness of these new ideas and activities often causes embarrassment, anxiety, and guilt that may lead to conflict with parents and other authority figures.

Middle school students feel a growing need for independence, self-identity, love, and a sense of belonging. The desire for the freedom and responsibility of an adult may lead to conflicts with adults as well as internal conflicts. Students of this age have a great need to be treated with respect in their drive toward adulthood. Ignoring or ridiculing this drive may cause students to look for acceptance in a less favorable way. They may rebel against the society that has failed them, that does not believe in them, or has hurt them in some way.

Adults often seem confused about how to relate to middle school students. They may treat them as children sometimes and as adults at other times. Such inconsistency can be confusing to adolescents. So what should we do?

# Establishing and Maintaining a Positive Learning Environment

> *"I enjoyed how you always encouraged me to try harder. Whenever I am at a ski race, I can hear your words in my head: 'Do your personal best; you did great, but next time try harder!' That made me think I could win the race, but even though I didn't, I felt good about myself."*
> —*Seventh grade student*

A positive learning environment takes into account the cognitive and affective as well as physical aspects of learning. Intrinsically motivated students find physical activity rewarding and fun and are less likely to engage in inappropriate behavior.

What are some of the things a teacher needs to do to establish a positive learning environment?

- Catch students being good—praise the specific behaviors you want to perpetuate.
- Accentuate the positive—emphasize what students do well rather than what they do incorrectly.
- Speak about the behaviors rather than the students.
- Treat all students positively—show an interest in them.

- Be an active listener—use eye contact and listen for hidden messages.
- Try to understand the students' points of view—don't prejudge.
- Be fair, consistent, accurate, and unemotional when addressing inappropriate behavior.
- Guide students in becoming responsible for their own actions and attitudes.
- Keep students physically active most of the lesson—that's what they expect, want, and need.
- Never preach, threaten, label, order, use sarcasm, or interrogate students.
- Don't think of disruptive behavior as a personal affront.
- Understand your feelings about the students—deal with negative feelings toward students in a private and positive manner as soon as possible.
- Routinely plan for and encourage student feedback through questions, discussions, and writings.
- Allow students to progress at their own rate much of the time.
- Learn every student's name as quickly as possible—don't hesitate to ask a student if you're not sure.
- Be organized.

Inappropriate behavior will occur from time to time, no matter how organized and positive you are. If the behavior is a minor infraction of short duration that does not interrupt the class, ignore it. Such behaviors include talking to a friend at an inappropriate time, daydreaming, or continuing an activity for a short time after you ask the class to stop. As long as the behavior is not a safety issue or a problem to other students, it's best not to interrupt your lesson to address it.

Recognizing appropriate behavior while ignoring inappropriate behavior is another method that can often be used effectively if not overdone. Positive attention maintains a warm atmosphere conducive to learning and emphasizes the desired behavior. Direct eye contact and nodding your head to a student engaged in inappropriate behavior is sometimes sufficient.

"I" messages can be an effective tool. You might say, "Class, I need your attention," "Billy, I need you to hold the ball still," or

"Barbara, I wonder if you understand the directions." Such messages address a minor transgression in a nonthreatening way, if you say them in a matter of fact manner.

Moving close to the offending student is another approach that is often quite effective. If the behavior doesn't improve by close proximity, add a personal "I" message: for example, "Joey, I need your full attention" or "Julie, I find it difficult to teach while you are bouncing the ball."

Borrowing the equipment of an offending student for demonstration purposes may be effective occasionally. When necessary, also add an "I" message. For example, if the student continues to talk after you took the equipment, say "Juanita, I need to have you stop talking while I explain what we are to do next." Again, make the messages unemotional, being especially careful not to express irritation.

Reminding the students what is expected of them before inappropriate behavior has occurred is often effective. This approach is particularly useful at transitional times, such as at the beginning of class, when getting equipment, when dividing into groups, or when leaving a play area.

Reacting positively should always be the first approach to inappropriate behavior. For students who continually disrupt the class and don't seem affected by positive intervention, you need to look beyond the overt behavior and figure out the cause. Is the student afraid of failing or looking foolish? Is the student trying to cover up an insecurity? Is the student looking for peer approval? The answer is not always obvious, but the student's behavior is most likely a way of dealing with a fear, insecurity, or need. To better understand the cause, you need more information from the student. Arrange a private meeting with the student when neither of you will feel rushed—perhaps before or after school. The purpose of the meeting is to ascertain candid information about why the student is reluctant to participate effectively. You might say, "Mary, you are usually enthusiastic, but you didn't show much effort today. Is there something I do that upsets you?" State the problem in a way that takes the focus off the student and makes the meeting less threatening. Listen to the student's response very carefully. Restate the student's response in you own words to verify the accuracy of your understanding. If your paraphrasing is correct, the student will feel validated and understood. If your interpretation is incorrect, the student has the opportunity to restate the concerns. Such interactions may help the student identify a fear, weakness, or need. Once identified, the student may eventually learn how to deal with it in a more positive way.

The student may also point out things that irritate or upset him/her that you do unconsciously. Accept any student criticism without taking it personally. If you feel the student criticism has merit, make a change in your teaching so you become more effective. If you believe the student criticism does not have merit, briefly explain what you are trying to accomplish and why. The value of such a meeting is for you to open up a dialogue, so that a better understanding of one another's feelings and concerns may develop. This is not a time for a lecture or for making threats of future punishment. The teacher who takes the time to meet, listen, and discuss the problem demonstrates respect for the student. This respect usually strengthens the relationship, whereas threats and lectures will destroy the rapport.

Once you and the student understand each other's views, you need to agree upon an appropriate course of action. Ask the student what changes she/he feels are necessary. If the student feels you are sincere about your concern for him/her as an individual, the response is likely to be positive and effective. If you feel the student's suggestions are unworkable, then you need to continue to develop a trusting and caring relationship with the student. Some behaviors may be the result of long-standing negative experiences, and trust may take time to develop.

It is easier to understand the behavior of students if you are in touch with your own feelings, insecurities, strengths, and weaknesses. Some common concerns of teachers include the fear of failure, exposing a weakness, looking foolish, or losing control of the class. Being aware of your shortcomings is the first step in improving your relationship with others.

> *"I have an apology to make to you. I am sorry for all the trouble I caused you when I was in middle school. I thank you for understanding me, being patient, and never screwing me to the wall."*
> *—26-year-old former student*

# Examples of Physical Education as a Positive and Enjoyable Experience

After I briefed the sixth grade students in their very first physical education class in September, Ben came up to me after class and quietly but in a serious tone said, "Mr. Hichwa, that was a good talk but, you know, I don't do gym." Ben informed me that he was cut from his fourth grade travel soccer team, his physical education experience in the elementary school was far from positive, and he did not intend to expose himself to further failure or ridicule in the sixth grade. In that very same class, Andrew brought his gym clothes in eager anticipation of starting a new physical education experience. He felt disappointment upon learning that the first meeting was only an informational one. Andrew's previous experiences in physical activities were very positive. He was on the state select soccer team and had played in many of the neighboring states. As their teacher, it was my responsibility to meet the needs of both of these students.

After class, I thanked Ben for being so forthright and suggested that he come to our next class as an observer, which he agreed to do. At the end of the class, I asked him if he thought he could feel comfortable taking part in future class activities. Because I took the time to listen to Ben, showed respect for his concerns, and gave him time to feel comfortable in his new environment, Ben agreed to give it a try! Throughout the year, Ben tried his best, participated fully, and eventually learned to enjoy the many challenges. It was the accepting atmosphere in the class that changed Ben's view of physical education. The experience had a profound affect on him that will likely remain throughout his life.

As for Andrew, he became an invaluable resource to the class. He was able to share some of the team drills he learned from his travel soccer experience. Teaching them to his classmates made him feel appreciated and important. He was a great example to the class not only for his proficiency in his skills, but also for his attitude and work ethic. He cheered his classmates and often asked a far less-accomplished student to be on his team. It was obvious how Andrew felt about his three years of middle school physical education when he approached me on the last day of school. I was alone in the gym when he walked across the floor, gave me a big hug, and said, "Thanks for everything, Mr. Hichwa." Andrew appreciated the opportunities he had to take on new challenges and the respect he received from doing them well.

Betsy began as a very quiet sixth grader. I hardly knew she was in class. Before long, however, I realized her skill level and knowledge of the activities were exceptional. She was cooperative, caring, competent, and competitive. She enjoyed new challenges but was very uncomfortable when attention focused on her. Even little comments like "Good job" or "Nice Shot" embarrassed her. Realizing how sensitive Betsy was about peer attention, I altered the manner in which I recognized her talents and attitudes. Whenever I had the opportunity, I would praise her privately. She appreciated my understanding and acceptance of her feelings. I believe it was because of our rapport that she was able to work to her potential.

In the eighth grade, Clare responded to the question, "How can you use what you have learned in physical education in other life situations?" She wrote:

> "I will always strive for the impossible. I won't say, 'I can't do this.' I'll say, 'I will give it a try.' I will never under estimate my ability by saying 'no' before I give it an honest effort. I will always push myself to do my very best."

That was not the Clare I knew at the beginning of her sixth grade year. She was very tall for her age, fairly heavy, and extremely clumsy. Clare would change her clothes and go through the motions, but even comments of encouragement from her peers were construed as personal affronts and caused her great anguish.

Because of her lack of skill, team sports activities proved to be Clare's toughest challenges. The small-group games we played gave her many opportunities to "touch" the ball, gain experience, and improve her skills. By making developmentally appropriate changes, the activities became less threatening. Clare started to experience a little success, and her self-concept was definitely on the rise.

Clare was very verbal and took risks with her opinions and suggestions. She excelled at the problem-solving initiatives and slowly gained respect from the other students by coming up with creative solutions. Running was a bigger challenge, though. Her times in the 50- and 100-meter runs were far from the best, but she would proudly record her times and work hard to improve those benchmarks. She didn't feel inadequate when competing against herself, and she enjoyed monitoring her progress. In the shot put, Clare had one of the best heaves in the class, and her pride was obvious. She no longer thought of herself as being unable to do anything well physically.

I encouraged Clare to play in the after-school intramural volleyball tournament in seventh grade. She accepted the challenge and enjoyed the experience. She became aware that all her efforts in class made her a more competent player in the tournament. For the first time, Clare learned what it was like to compete on a team, and she relished it.

By eighth grade, Clare felt confident enough to demonstrate the layup shot in basketball! Her fitness scores and times in various running events improved dramatically. She was more skilled, more fit, and felt better about herself. I believe her new attitude about physical activity will result in a healthier lifestyle throughout her life.

Toward the end of the school year, I asked Clare to write about her feelings and to respond to the following question:

> "What have you done thus far that you feel particularly proud of?"

She wrote:

> "To tell you the truth, I'm proud of a lot of things that I've done. However, I'm most proud of my climbing achievements in the Project Adventure class. When I was in sixth and even in seventh grade, I was terrified of climbing. I could not believe that I was being asked to buckle myself to a rope and then asked to scale a wall. I was terrified.
>
> "But in eighth grade, I climbed the wall and a tree. I did the zip line, soaring through the sky past several trees. Then, the ultimate challenge, I went rock climbing and scaled a rock face. Above it all, I had fun doing it. God, have I changed.
>
> "I also want to say that our physical education and adventure programs enable the students to discover a lot about ourselves. I personally discovered that I under-rated my abilities. I will always push myself a little harder. I will never forget how much fun I had in class and what it meant to me to have the entire class cheering me on."

Teaching middle school youngsters is always a challenge. They will respect you for being well prepared for your classes, for having interesting and appropriate activities to teach, and for treating each of them with respect. Because it is a difficult transitional period in their lives, their behavior will not always be rational. They will not always act maturely and be a positive role model. It may also help to look at yourself in the mirror each morning before you head off for work and say, "No middle school student is going to ruin my day today!" Never underestimate the value of a sense of humor.

# 2nd Inning

# Planning

## Yearly, Unit, and Daily Physical Education Plans

> *"There is no 'secret' to being a successful communicator—just prepare, know your subject, and care."*
> —Leo Buscaglia

Planning is essential for mapping where you hope to go and how you plan to get there. When you formulate your curriculum objectives, include the social and emotional needs of your students as well as the skills to be taught. Give serious thought to the attitudes and behaviors you wish to cultivate in your students and how you plan to nurture them.

The type of environment you create will influence the learning that will take place. Therefore, your first consideration should be how to create a safe physical education environment where all students feel accepted, appreciated, and respected for who they are. Establish rules that make clear to every student which behaviors are acceptable and which are not. Write your rules on a poster board and prominently display them in the gym for reference throughout the year. As situations arise, take advantage of that teachable moment to reinforce the attitudes and behaviors you wish to foster.

Your rules could be the three Rs, as described in the third inning, or you may devise your own. Your goals are to safeguard students from emotional damage, promote positive student attitudes, and make physical activity so enjoyable that it becomes part of every student's lifestyle.

## Building a Yearly Plan

Once you have established the rules for creating a safe emotional environment, your next step is to decide which activities and sports you wish to teach throughout the year. Make a list of all the sports and activities you would consider including in your progressive curriculum. Take into consideration your time allotment (length and frequency of class meetings), equipment and space availability, class size, student skill levels and interests, other programs offered in town, and likely weather conditions (outside vs. inside). Be sure that what you include is developmentally appropriate and progressive for each grade level you teach.

Here are some of the sports and activities you may want to include:

| | | |
|---|---|---|
| keep-away activities | pickle ball | juggling activities |
| volleyball | touch football | takraw |
| softball | floor hockey | field hockey |
| soccer | rounders | track-and-field activities |
| basketball | school rugby | cross-country |
| badminton | dance | gymnastics |
| team handball | cricket | fitness testing |
| conditioning activities | lacrosse | Project Adventure activities |

Once you have listed all the sports and other activities you will consider including in your yearly curriculum, decide in what part of the school year you will teach each activity, how many class periods you will devote to each, and how to make your curriculum progressive for the grades you teach.

The yearly plan I used at the John Read Middle School is shown in the form that follows. The plan lists the activities presented and the approximate amount of time spent on each. At the John Read Middle School, students have physical education every other day throughout the year. Project Adventure is a separate program which sixth and seventh graders take for one quarter (approximately 22 sessions) and the eighth grade students take for half of the year (approximately 44 sessions). A health class is also part of each student's curriculum. Dance is offered as a unit, but line dances and upper-arm-strength activities are performed as warm-up activities throughout the year. More information about Project Adventure can be found in the extra-inning section at the end of this book.

## John Read Middle School Physical Education Program

| Major Area | Grade 6 | Grade 7 | Grade 8 |
|---|---|---|---|
| First marking period—9 weeks | | | |
| Keep-away activities (2 weeks) | Basic throwing, catching, moving with and without the ball | ➡ | |
| | 2-on-1, 2-on-2, 3-on-2, 3-on-3 | ➡ | ➡ |
| | Ultimate keep-away (using different implements) | ➡ | ➡ |

*(continued)*

*(continued)*

# John Read Middle School
# Physical Education Program

| Major Area | Grade 6 | Grade 7 | Grade 8 |
|---|---|---|---|
| Team sports (5 weeks) | Soccer | ⇒ | ⇒ |
| | Team handball | ⇒ | ⇒ |
| | | Lacrosse | ⇒ |
| | | Field hockey | ⇒ |
| | | Touch football | ⇒ |
| | | | School rugby |
| Cross-country (1 week) | Training activities, cross-country meet | ⇒ | ⇒ |
| Physical-fitness testing (1 week) | Fitness gram | ⇒ | ⇒ |
| Second and third marking period—18 weeks | | | |
| Dance (two weeks) | Line dance | ⇒ | ⇒ |
| Team sports | Basketball (4 weeks) | ⇒ | ⇒ |
| | Volleyball (4 weeks) | ⇒ | ⇒ |
| | Floor hockey (2 weeks) | ⇒ | ⇒ |
| | Indoor team handball (2 weeks) | ⇒ | ⇒ |

| Major Area | Grade 6 | Grade 7 | Grade 8 |
|---|---|---|---|
| Juggling skills (2 weeks) | Scarf and ball juggling | ⟶ | ⟶ |
|  | Spinning plates | ⟶ | ⟶ |
|  | Diablo devil sticks | ⟶ | ⟶ |
| Conditioning (2 weeks) | Walking | ⟶ | ⟶ |
|  | Aerobic vs. anaerobic exercises | ⟶ | ⟶ |
|  | Circuit training | ⟶ | ⟶ |
|  | Using heart rate monitors | ⟶ | ⟶ |
|  | Self-testing activities | ⟶ | ⟶ |
| Fourth marking period—8 weeks | | | |
| Track-and-field (4 weeks) | 50 m dash | 100 m dash | 400 m run |
|  | Running long jump | ⟶ | ⟶ |
|  | Triple jump | ⟶ | ⟶ |
|  | 4 x 100 relay | ⟶ | ⟶ |
|  | High jump | ⟶ | ⟶ |
|  | 50 m hurdles | ⟶ | ⟶ |
|  | 6 lb. shot | Discus | 5/8 lb. shot |

(continued)

*(continued)*

# John Read Middle School
# Physical Education Program

| Major Area | Grade 6 | Grade 7 | Grade 8 |
|---|---|---|---|
| Striking skills (4 weeks) | Paddle/foam ball | ⠂⠂➡ | Paddle/ foam/ "pickle ball" |
| | Softball (one base) | Softball (6-on-6) | |
| | | Golf | ⠂⠂➡ |
| | | Rounders | Badminton |
| | | | Cricket |

When building a yearly plan, it is important to

- work with your strengths,
- provide activities that stress teamwork and personal fitness, and
- keep a constant check on the community programs offered.

No one plan is perfect and no one activity is indispensable. Keep the offerings interesting for both you and the students.

# Unit Planning

After you have decided what to include in your yearly curriculum, as well as when, how long, and at what grade level, you are ready to begin preparing your unit plans.

Each unit will have three main components: objectives, action plan, and assessment of student progress. These components are outlined in the following diagram.

## Three Main Components of a Unit Plan

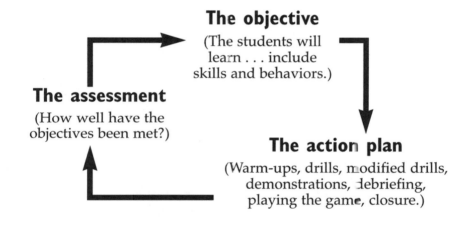

**The objective**
(The students will learn . . . include skills and behaviors.)

**The assessment**
(How well have the objectives been met?)

**The action plan**
(Warm-ups, drills, modified drills, demonstrations, debriefing, playing the game, closure.)

For the objectives of each unit, ask yourself what specific skills and behaviors you want the students to learn and consistently demonstrate. For example, if the unit is keep-away, you might include the following objectives for the students to learn:

- The proper techniques for throwing and catching while stationary and while moving
- How and when to use offensive and defensive techniques
- How to coach their peers in keep-away activities
- To include every class member as an integral part of the game
- To treat every class member with respect
- To be responsible for the proper care of the equipment

Once you have determined your objectives, incorporate them into your action plan in a progressive manner. In the game of keep-away, one of the initial objectives is for the students to learn the proper techniques of throwing and catching while stationary and while moving. To meet that objective, list specific activities you might use to teach those skills. Organize the activities in a progressive manner, reflecting the order they are to be taught. Be realistic about the amount of time you have in each class, so as to keep each lesson varied and interesting. Continually evaluate student performance and make adjustments accordingly. For example, if the students need more practice learning the basic skills of throwing and catching, you need to spend more time practicing those skills. If the students are reasonably skilled at throwing and catching, more of the class time may be better spent in a variety of play situations.

Organize each objective by listing specific ways you plan to teach the objective in a progressive manner. Decide when and how each objective will be introduced into the unit and how you plan to evaluate how well the objective is being met.

The assessment of your objectives may be done in a variety of ways. Some effective ways include group debriefings, skill testing, written tests, student writing samples, and teacher observation. One of the values of assessment is that it can offer the teacher a better understanding of how well the objectives are being met and whether or not changes need to be made in the action plan. Assessment can also help focus student attention on the objectives. It helps students become more aware of what the goals are and how well they are doing to meet them. Records of student performance can provide a benchmark by which students can monitor their progress.

Debriefing may be done at any time in the unit. It may consist of a single question to focus attention on a single objective, or it may include a number of questions about topics you want the students to think about.

Student skills may be evaluated by the teacher, by pairs of students testing one another, or by students testing themselves and recording their own results on a paper provided by the teacher for that purpose.

Written tests are useful to help you evaluate how well students understand what you have covered in class. Such a test may cover such concepts as the rules of the game, strategy, signals used by umpires, and history of the game.

Writing samples are useful for teacher feedback concerning student knowledge, feelings, and concerns. Often students hide their true feelings to protect themselves. A perceptive teacher can word a question in such a way that students feel free to express themselves without concern for peer appraisal.

# Daily Lesson Planning

A well-planned lesson allows you to focus on the students rather than on what to do next or how to keep the class involved and under control. If you concentrate on student interactions, you are likely to be more flexible in adjusting the lesson to the students' needs and their abilities. No matter how well you plan, some lessons won't go the way you expect. Some aspects of the lesson may be too difficult, while others may not be challenging enough. The lesson may fail to elicit much enthusiasm, or it may be an unexpected hit. Proper planning helps you quickly adjust the lesson but still keep a proper sequence.

Thoughtful and creative planning is essential for smooth transitions from one activity to another and for maintaining a positive atmosphere that encourages learning. A well-planned lesson maximizes activity and minimizes teacher talk. A physically challenging lesson increases the probability of appropriate student behavior, maximizes skill development, and is more fun. A well-thought-out lesson makes teaching a more rewarding experience for all involved.

When developing the daily lesson plans, consider the personalities and skill levels of individual students and of classes as a whole. Form a vision of what you want your students to learn. Before you begin, consider

- the objectives of the lesson,
- the entering skill levels of the students,
- the basic skills that need to be reviewed,
- the warm-ups that are most appropriate,
- the drills and demonstrations to use,
- the necessary equipment,
- the most appropriate organization of the students.

- the amount of time to be spent on developing skills,
- the amount of time to be spent playing the game,
- the plan for debriefing and/or closure, and
- appropriate ways that you and your students can assess progress.

> "Physical education teachers and coaches will not become experts in their fields simply by reading articles. It takes experience and practice, in addition to knowledge, to reach the pinnacle of expert. Even when teachers and coaches have sufficient knowledge and experience they may never become truly expert in their chosen callings. In the study of experts it has been discovered that those who reach the top of their field never stopped learning and never stopped trying to be the best they could be."
> —Dr. Paul G. Schempp, professor in the Curriculum and Instruction Research Laboratory at the University of Georgia–Athens.

# Beginning Activity

Get students actively involved as quickly as possible. You can accomplish this by having the students do a line dance, stretches, jogging, upper-arm strength activities, or appropriate drills.

# Sharing the Objectives of the Lesson

Once the students have gotten their hearts pumping from a vigorous warm-up, explain what the focus of the day's lesson will be. It can go something like this:

> "We will be learning and practicing the proper techniques of throwing and catching while stationary and while moving. You will have a new partner each time the activity changes."

# Practicing Drills and Playing Modified Games (Demonstration and Practice)

To develop skills required for specific games and activities, you should devote much of the class time to practice in drills and modified games in which participation is at a maximum. The rules of the games should be modified to accommodate the skill level and experience of the students. Teams should be limited to three-to-six students.

# Assessment

The assessment for an activity may include teacher observation, skill tests, debriefings, and written responses to teacher-generated questions.

While observing the students throwing and catching, ask yourself questions such as the following:

- Do the students know where to aim a pass so that a moving receiver can catch it?
- Are the students moving to an open space to receive a pass?
- How well are the students working together?

- How well do the students understand and follow instructions?
- Are their throwing and catching skills improving?
- Are they enthusiastic and enjoying the game?

Change your action plan when necessary as you observe the students' behavior and skill proficiency.

In many activities your observation is adequate to determine the skill level of a class. A skill test is useful to more accurately assess how well each individual student can perform a specific skill. Skill tests give students immediate feedback about their proficiency to perform the skill tested. That information may be used as a benchmark for students to monitor their progress in learning the skill. Students may pair off and test one another reciprocally, or you may provide a sheet of paper on which students record their own results. Students are often highly motivated to work on improving their own scores on a skill test and should be given plenty of opportunities to do so. See game #1, sixth inning, for examples of skill tests. Keep in mind that the purpose of the skill test is not grading. Its value is to inform the students about how well they can perform a specific task and to motivate them to be self-responsible for improving that skill.

Debriefing is a very effective way to assess a class's knowledge, feelings, and concerns. Facilitating a debriefing takes practice to do well, but it is worth the effort it takes to learn. Sample debriefing questions to use in a keep-away unit may include the following:

- Who would like to describe the most efficient way to throw?
- Where should you aim when throwing to a moving target?
- What are some good catching techniques?
- How can a receiver get free from an opponent?
- What are some of the things you can do to intercept a ball?
- How can you defend your opponent?
- What role do respect and responsibility play in testing your partner?
- What did you like or dislike about working with a partner?
- What can we do to keep the equipment in good condition?

Only one or two questions should be asked in each debriefing. Keep debriefings brief! Focus on only one or two points, and then get the students moving again. See game #1, seventh inning, for more information about how to debrief.

Some students are apprehensive about verbally sharing their feelings and concerns with their peers. Many find it easier to express themselves in writing. Since you teach many students in a day, be selective about which classes and how many classes you ask to respond to a question in writing. You want to gain information by reading their responses carefully, discuss the results with the class sampled, and make adjustments in your teaching as needed. Think carefully about what you want to learn from the students sampled. Ask only one or two questions per writing sample. It should take no more than five minutes for the students to respond, and it is generally best to have them write at the end of an active class.

Listed below are examples of questions you might ask:

---

Did you enjoy the activity? Why or why not?

How well did your team work together? Give examples.

Did you learn anything new about guarding your opponent or freeing yourself from one? Explain.

What value do you think this activity has?

If you were the teacher, what would you do differently?

---

## Closure

A few minutes before dismissal time, highlight a positive happening, briefly review what was accomplished in the class, and inform the students about what they will be doing in the next class. This closure process helps students become more aware of what is expected of them and what to look forward to. Such a closure also helps the students settle down, catch their breath, and lower their excitement levels, so they can change their clothes and go to their next class in a more relaxed mode.

## Involving the Students When Introducing a New Unit

Before beginning a new unit, brainstorm with the students about what they expect to learn in the unit. Write their responses on a blackboard. Ask questions to help them focus, if needed. Spend no more than five to ten minutes doing this activity.

A brainstorming session on keep-away may go something like this:

**Teacher:** We will be playing keep-away for the next four classes. What do we need to know in order to play keep-away successfully?

**Student responses:**

- How to throw and catch
- Where to move with and without the ball
- How to play defense
- The rules
- How to work as a team

**Teacher:** Good job! In your next four physical education classes, we will be

- practicing throwing and catching,
- playing a variety of keep-away games, and
- playing Ultimate Keep-Away.

**Student response:** How much time will we be playing the game?

**Teacher:** That depends on how quickly you learn the skills necessary to play. When you consistently throw and catch successfully and work well as a team, we'll start playing the game.

# Sample Daily Lesson Plans

Following are four lesson plans. They may be used as a guide for planning your own.

## Sample Daily Lesson Plan #1

**Grade:** 6

**Unit topic:** keep-away

**Topic of the day:** lead-up activities for keep-away

**Focus of the lesson:** throwing and catching

**Equipment needed:** a variety of throwing objects, such as junior-sized footballs, Frisbees, rubber chickens, Spider Balls, intermediate- (or smaller-sized) basketballs, rugby balls—one throwing object for every two students

**Sharing the objectives of the lesson:** We will be practicing the proper techniques of throwing and catching while stationary and while moving.

**Beginning activity:** Find a partner who is approximately the same height as you are and pick out an object to be thrown. Start about 10 yards apart and practice throwing and catching with one another. (Please note: Always have a designated spot where students can go if they choose not to pick a partner or can't find one. It's a "safety circle," and you can pair up those students who need a partner.)

**Demonstration #1:** A stationary student throws to a stationary receiver. Point out how the leg opposite the throwing arm steps forward and the weight is transferred forward as the object is thrown.

**Practice #1:** Students throw and catch in pairs, coaching each other in the proper technique as necessary.

**Demonstration #2:** A stationary student throws to a moving receiver. Point out that the ball should be thrown in front of the moving receiver.

**Practice #2:** Throwers stand still as they throw to their moving partners. Partners coach one another as necessary.

**Demonstration #3:** A thrower moves and throws to a stationary partner.

**Practice #3:** Throwers move while they throw to their stationary partners. Partners coach one another as necessary.

**Demonstration #4:** A thrower moves and throws to a moving partner.

**Practice #4:** Throwers move as they throw to moving partners.

**Demonstration #5:** A receiver fakes in one direction and then moves in the opposite direction to receive a pass. Point out where the thrower should aim.

**Practice #5:** Students practice faking one way and then moving in the opposite direction while receiving an object from their partners. Partners coach one another.

**Debriefing:** Students form a semicircle around you. Debrief by asking such questions as:

a. Why should you lead with the opposite foot when you throw?

b. Can you name the five throwing and catching fundamentals we worked on today?

c. Where should you aim when throwing to a moving receiver?

**Closure:** Point out positive happenings. Tell the students that their next class will begin with basic throwing and catching fundamentals with a new partner!

## Sample Daily Lesson Plan #2

**Grade:** 6

**Unit topic:** keep-away

**Topic of the day:** offensive and defensive techniques

**Focus of the lesson:** lead-up games to keep-away

**Equipment needed:** a variety of throwing objects, such as junior-sized footballs, Frisbees, rubber chickens, Spider Balls, intermediate- (or smaller-sized) basketballs, rugby balls—one throwing object for every two students

**Sharing the objectives of the lesson:** We will be practicing offensive and defensive techniques while playing keep-away.

**Beginning activity:** Work on the four basic throwing and catching fundamentals we practiced in the last class. Find a partner who was born in the same month as you were.

**Demonstration #1:** Two-on-one. Two students attempt to keep an object away from a third student. Discuss possible strategies of offense and defense.

**Practice #1:** Students get into groups of three and play two-on-one. When the defensive person touches the object or when seven passes are successfully completed, the players change positions.

**Demonstration #2:** One-on-one with two "posts." Two students play one-on-one within a grid, and two students act as "posts" outside the grid. The goal for the offensive player is to receive a pass outside the end line from one of the "post" players. If successful, a point is scored. The defensive player tries to intercept the pass.

**Practice #2:** Students get into groups of four and practice playing one-on-one with two "posts," as demonstrated. On the teacher-specified signal, the "posts" and players exchange places—every 30 to 45 seconds.

**Playing the game:** Have each group of students decide the size of their grid. Play two-on-two. A point is scored if the throwing object is caught over the end grid line. The object goes to the defensive team after a point is scored.

**Debriefing:** Students form a semicircle around you. Debrief by asking such questions as:

a. Where should you position yourself to keep your opponent from receiving the throwing object?
b. What do you need to do to create space when you are on the offensive?
c. In what ways can offensive and defensive players communicate?

**Closure:** Point out positive happenings. Tell the students their next class will begin with games of two-on-two.

## Sample Daily Lesson Plan #3

**Grade:** 6

**Unit topic:** keep-away

**Topic of the day:** reviewing offensive and defensive strategies

**Focus of the lesson:** using students as coaches

**Equipment needed:** a variety of throwing objects, such as junior-sized footballs, Frisbees, rubber chickens, Spider Balls, intermediate- (or smaller-) sizes basketballs—one throwing object for two students; small cones to be used as goals

**Sharing the objectives of the lesson:** There will be a "student coach" at each station today. That student will be responsible for helping anyone in the group who has a question or needs more instruction in how to execute offensive and defensive movement strategies.

> **Beginning activity:** Students get into groups of four and play two-on-two. See if the offensive team can complete 10 passes in succession.
>
> **Demonstration #1:** One-on-one with two "posts" and a coach. Review how to play one-on-one with the aid of two "posts." Model coaching techniques by reminding the offensive players to move to an open space and fake one way then move in the opposite direction. Coach the defensive players to stay close to the opponent they are guarding and keep their eyes on the throwing object.
>
> **Practice #1:** Students get into groups of five. Play one-on-one with two "posts" and a coach. Students rotate positions on your signal.
>
> **Demonstration #2:** Three-on-three. Play three-on-three with no boundaries. When you begin, add the rule that players may not pass the object to the teammate they received it from. The defensive players go on offense when they intercept the ball or when the offense completes 10 passes in succession.
>
> **Practice #2:** Students get into groups of six and play three-on-three with no boundaries.
>
> **Demonstration #3:** Play three-on-three with you modeling coaching techniques.
>
> **Practice #3:** Students get into groups of seven to play three-on-three with a coach. Students rotate positions on your signal.
>
> **Debriefing:** Students form a semicircle around you. Debrief by asking such questions as:

a. How were the coaches helpful?

b. How did students respond to the coaches' suggestions?

c. What can students do to become better coaches?

**Closure:** Point out positive happenings. Tell the students their next class will begin by playing games of three-on-three.

## Sample Daily Lesson Plan #4

**Grade:** 6

**Unit topic:** keep-away

**Topic of the day:** playing ultimate keep-away

**Focus of the lesson:** making everyone an intricate part of the game

**Equipment needed:** a variety of throwing objects, such as junior-sized footballs, Frisbees, rubber chickens, Spider Balls, intermediate- (or smaller-sized) basketballs—one throwing object for every six players; small cones to be used as goals

**Sharing the objectives of the lesson:** Work together in such a way that every student becomes an integral part of the game.

**Beginning activity:** Students get into groups of six and play three-on-three. Each team tries to complete 10 passes in succession.

**Demonstration #1:** Play three-on-three within a grid and with a goal line at each end of the grid. Each team tries to successfully pass the object to a teammate who is over the opponents' goal line. The rules are as follows:

1. No body contact is allowed.
2. You may take three steps with the object.
3. If the object touches the ground, is intercepted by an opponent, or a point is scored, the opposing team gets the object.

4. The defender may guard the opponent. If the offensive person with the object has not taken three steps, that person may move, but the defender may not. If the offensive person has taken three steps, the defender may stay on the offensive player.

**Playing the game #1:** Students get into groups of six and play three-on-three with goals.

**Demonstration #2:** Demonstrate how to create an open space by faking one way and moving another way. Add the rule that each teammate must score before a player can score a second goal.

**Playing the game #2:** Continue playing three-on-three with the added rule and encourage the students to use the faking techniques demonstrated.

**Debriefing:** Students form a semicircle around you. Debrief by asking such questions as:

a. How did you feel about the rules?
b. Can you think of a way to imrove the game?
c. How did your team work together?
d. What have you learned by playing keep-away?

**Closure:** Point out positive behaviors you observed. Inform the students that they will begin a soccer unit in their next class.

> *"I go knowing that the plans I have carefully laid out on paper or in my mind's eye are surely destined to be altered. I would be terribly disappointed and surprised if my ideas were not reshaped by the students they were designed to teach."*
> —*George Hochsprung, seventh grade math teacher, Rogers Park Middle School, Danbury, CT*

# 3rd Inning

# Including the Three Rs in Physical Education

> **Internalizing the three Rs can help students meet the following content standards:**
>
> 5. Demonstrates responsible personal and social behavior in physical-activity settings.
> 6. Demonstrates understanding and respect for differences among people in physical-activity settings.
> 7. Understands that physical activity provides opportunities for enjoyment, challenge, self-expression, and social interaction.

When asked what I teach, I like to respond, "Children." Teaching physical skills is an important responsibility of a physical education teacher, but even more important is nurturing prosocial behaviors. Teachers should not expect students to be intuitively respectful, responsible, or resourceful, any more than they should expect them to adequately develop their physical skills on their own. The best physical education teachers consciously include activities that facilitate the development of physical skills while also nurturing the attitudes of respect and responsibility.

As a teacher, you set the tone of the class. If, in your classes, you are warm and supportive of individual differences, the behavior of your students will reflect that. Only in such an atmosphere can respect and responsibility flourish. Students must feel respected for who they are—regardless of their physical prowess, size, weight, or nationality—before they can be expected to be responsible.

Students who consistently demonstrate respectful and responsible behavior are more likely to possess the creative and problem-solving skills necessary to be resourceful. Physical education activities, by their very nature, provide endless opportunities for students to learn, cultivate, and practice being resourceful. Every game involves making quick decisions, cooperating with others, solving problems, and communicating through words and actions. Cooperative games, initiatives, and dance activities also provide many opportunities to be resourceful. Teaching the three Rs of respect, responsibility, and resourcefulness is not an easy task, but through careful planning, it can be successfully accomplished. Your students will be better prepared to deal successfully with life's many challenges if the three Rs have become internalized.

*Webster's* defines "respect," "responsibility," and "resourcefulness" in the following ways (see box).

---

**Respect**

- to show consideration for
- to feel or show honor or esteem for

**Responsibility**

- condition, quality, fact, or instance of being responsible
- obligation, accountability, dependability
- responsible . . . able to distinguish between right and wrong and to think and act rationally, and hence accountable for one's behavior

**Resourcefulness**

- a means of accomplishing something
- a source of strength or ability within oneself
- ability to deal promptly and effectively with problems and difficulties

Those are good definitions, but teachers need something more specific to guide their students. I use the following three Rs for my students. Make up your own three Rs, display them prominently in your gymnasium, and refer to them frequently throughout the year.

## Three Rs for the Students

**Respect**

- Be thoughtful.
- Be helpful.
- Use good listening skills.
- Be willing to share and take turns.
- Accept others as they are.
- Accept and follow rules.
- Talk in a friendly manner.
- Call each other by name.

**Responsibility**

- Answer for your own behavior.
- Take good care of the equipment.
- Stay physically fit.
- Remember your gym clothes.
- Follow directions.
- Try your best.
- Be honest and fair.
- Be cooperative.
- Evaluate yourself fairly.

**Resourcefulness**

- Share your ideas when appropriate.
- Figure out ways to improve your skills.
- Work up to your potential.
- Set personal goals and strategies to meet them.
- Be creative.
- Be an effective problem solver.

The posted three Rs make clear to the students what is expected of them. Posting the three Rs is helpful, but you must also make them the basis of your lesson plans and part of your daily dialogue with the students.

"Do as I say, not as I do" doesn't work! The teacher as a role model is one of the most effective tools for teaching social skills. The teacher's responsibilities are different from the students', so I devised the three Rs for teachers. Read them carefully and then look critically at you own teaching style and make changes where warranted.

# Three Rs for the Teachers

## Respect

- Always speak courteously.
- Accept individual differences.
- Recognize positive behavior often.
- Include the students in the decision-making process periodically.
- Listen carefully to what students have to say.
- Eliminate elimination games.
- Have no human-target games.
- Use a whistle only when refereeing.
- Learn every student's name.

## Responsibility

- Understand child development.
- Be organized.
- Plan thoroughly, taking the needs of the whole child into consideration.
- Be consistent and fair.
- Cultivate a warm and caring environment.
- Provide developmentally appropriate equipment.
- Plan for maximum participation.
- Stay physically fit.

## Resourcefulness

- Create opportunities for students to chart their own progress and be self-responsible.
- Provide challenges for students to work at their own level frequently.
- Include motivating music when appropriate.
- Vary your warm-ups for interest and motivation.
- Keep drills progressive, challenging, varied, and fun.
- Plan opportunities for student creativity.
- Think of meaningful ways to include parents.
- Use innovative equipment.
- Provide opportunities for teacher-student interactions.

Some physical education teachers have been known to have a different set of three Rs. Their three Rs would be "to take Roll," "Roll out the ball," and "Read the newspaper." I hope to eliminate those three Rs in favor of "respect," "responsibility," and "resourcefulness."

The teacher who is a good role model for the three Rs and has established a positive learning environment in which students regularly demonstrate respect, responsibility, and resourcefulness can depend on the class to work effectively independently. The teacher can work with one group while the rest of the class is actively involved and working on its own! Small-group interaction personalizes teaching and is a strong motivational tactic.

The following illustrations are examples of two groups of students being self-responsible, for example, "calling" their own game, keeping score, and seeing that every student is contributing and playing. The third group is being monitored by the teacher, who has the opportunity to personalize instruction by giving specific suggestions to each student regarding skills, behavior, team play, and use of strategy. I have found it very satisfying as a teacher to have three or more groups working independently and effectively.

**Group 1:** The small group of students pictured below is playing a variation of round ball. For more information on this game, see page 158.

**Group 2:** Another group of students, pictured in figure 10, is playing keep-away. The group is working independently, including refereeing its own game.

**Group 3:** The teacher in the figure below is working with a third group of students, giving individual instruction and adding variations to the activity.

Individualizing instruction and giving students the opportunity and the responsibility to play on their own are effective strategies only when most of the students are consistently respectful and responsible. Small groups working independently allow all students to be actively involved as much as possible. Small groups allow the teacher to personalize instruction given to the students in one group while the other groups are working independently.

# 4th Inning

# Grading in Physical Education

## A Collaborative Effort Between Students and Teacher

> **When students have the opportunity to grade themselves they are more likely to exhibit the following content standard:**
> 5. Demonstrates responsible personal and social behavior in physical-activity settings.

In the beginning of the school year, inform your students that they will be grading themselves in physical education each marking period. They will be given the opportunity to give their input to determine the criteria for grading. The criteria must make it possible for every student to earn an A regardless of athletic ability. You will use their input to form grading criteria for all students. The criteria will be posted in the gymnasium as a reminder throughout the year.

Obtain student ideas by conducting a debriefing session with each class. Begin the debrief by asking, "What criteria do you think your grade in physical education should be based on, with the possibility of every student earning an A?" Common student responses include

- working hard,
- being nice to others,
- following rules,
- trying your best, and
- listening to the teacher.

The criteria students think are important are generally the same you would use to determine a student's grade. If the students don't cover all the areas you think are important, initiate responses in those areas. You might ask, "What about the care of equipment?" or, "What role should improvement play in the grading criteria?"

Tell the students that their grades will be based on how frequently they display the behaviors they agreed are important in physical education. Write the criteria the students have established for grading on a poster and display the poster prominently in the gymnasium. Periodically ask the students at the end of the class how they felt they did during the class, based on the grading criteria. Frequently cite examples of how students worked hard, cooperated, gave support to others, and demonstrated a caring attitude. Promote the grading system in a very positive manner and **never use it as a threat.**

At the end of the marking period, review the grading criteria with each class. Explain that they are to give themselves an

---

**A** if the criteria were demonstrated on a consistent basis,

**B** if the criteria were usually met, or

**C** if the criteria were inconsistently met.

---

The following chart is an example of what the grading criteria might look like.

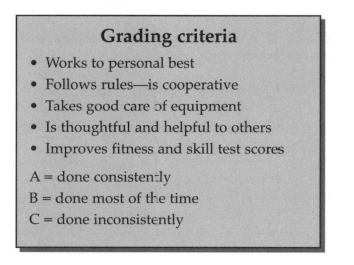

## Grading criteria

- Works to personal best
- Follows rules—is cooperative
- Takes good care of equipment
- Is thoughtful and helpful to others
- Improves fitness and skill test scores

A = done consistently
B = done most of the time
C = done inconsistently

Give the students a 5-inch x 7-inch card to record their grade and to write a paragraph explaining why they think they deserve that grade. You should grade each student independently as well, based on the same criteria.

The vast majority of students will grade themselves accurately. Of those who don't, it is more common for them to grade themselves too low rather than too high. If there is a discrepancy between the student's and the teacher's evaluation, arrange a time to meet with the student to discuss it. If a student is consistently disrespectful, irresponsible, or lacking motivation, it's essential that the underlying reason for such behavior be identified and addressed. For more information about how to deal with such problems, refer to Game #1, 1st Inning.

Since physical education teachers see a great many students and it is impossible to accurately remember how each student behaved over the course of a marking period, some type of tracking system needs to be devised. This is important not only to determine a fair grade for each student, but also to defend it. Use a system to document specifically what a student is or is not doing in class.

The form that follows presents a system you might find helpful. It can be used for taking attendance as well as keeping a record of student behaviors. Place an A next to the name of any student who is absent. Place a number next to those students you wish to track, corresponding to the behaviors listed in the upper right corner of the page. If the behavior was negative, place a minus sign next to the number. Record exceptional behavior as well as inappropriate behavior. Use the bottom part of the page to record a more detailed description of the behavior, when desired.

## Physical Education Class List

Grade _____

Class _____

Activity _____

Date

1 –Works and tries hard
2 –Follows rules
3 –Respects equipment
4 –Respectful of others
5 –Caring and helpful to others

| # | Name | | | | | | | | | | | | | |
|---|------|--|--|--|--|--|--|--|--|--|--|--|--|--|
| 1 | | | | | | | | | | | | | | |
| 2 | | | | | | | | | | | | | | |
| 3 | | | | | | | | | | | | | | |
| 4 | | | | | | | | | | | | | | |
| 5 | | | | | | | | | | | | | | |
| 6 | | | | | | | | | | | | | | |
| 7 | | | | | | | | | | | | | | |
| 8 | | | | | | | | | | | | | | |
| 9 | | | | | | | | | | | | | | |
| 10 | | | | | | | | | | | | | | |
| 11 | | | | | | | | | | | | | | |
| 12 | | | | | | | | | | | | | | |
| 13 | | | | | | | | | | | | | | |
| 14 | | | | | | | | | | | | | | |
| 15 | | | | | | | | | | | | | | |
| 16 | | | | | | | | | | | | | | |
| 17 | | | | | | | | | | | | | | |
| 18 | | | | | | | | | | | | | | |
| 19 | | | | | | | | | | | | | | |
| 20 | | | | | | | | | | | | | | |
| 21 | | | | | | | | | | | | | | |
| 22 | | | | | | | | | | | | | | |
| 23 | | | | | | | | | | | | | | |
| 24 | | | | | | | | | | | | | | |
| 25 | | | | | | | | | | | | | | |

Notes:
9/3 J. Rodriguez helped Mike correct his throwing motion.
9/3 M. Doe threw the ball to the other end of the gym when asked to put it away.

The goal of this grading system is to help students become responsible for their own behavior and to encourage them to reach out to others. With this system, it is possible for a gifted athlete to get a B or even a C for a grade. Skill and conditioning assessment are important, as is evaluating student knowledge of physical education topics and concepts. However, the most important goals of a middle school physical education program are to help students become self-responsible, empathetic, cooperative, honest, and self-motivated. With only these goals in your grading criteria, every student is capable of earning an A, and any student who consistently works to his or her potential and is responsible and caring deserves one! It is the teacher's responsibility to teach and assess the appropriate skills and physical activities in an environment conducive to developing the behaviors listed in the grading criteria.

# 5th Inning

# Writing in Physical Education

> **Carefully worded questions for students to respond to in writing can help them meet the following content standards:**
>
> 2. Applies movement concepts and principles to the learning and development of motor skills.
> 5. Demonstrates responsible personal and social behavior in physical-activity settings.
> 6. Demonstrates understanding and respect for differences among people in physical-activity settings.

Select a class to provide a writing sample and allow the students the last five minutes or so of class time to respond to a question on which you would like feedback. The question should require more than a one-word answer. The following questions/statements are the type I found useful:

- What did you find challenging in today's lesson?
- What did you find frustrating in today's lesson?
- Did you feel the teacher was well prepared? Why or why not?
- What do you think the teacher could have done differently to improve the lesson?
- Name three things you learned today, two things you particularly enjoyed, and one thing you can improve upon.
- Did you observe anyone helping another student in class? Describe how.
- Name as many sports as you can think of in which the ready position is used.
- What strategies are used in playing the game of keep-away?
- Why are warm-ups important before participating in aerobic activities?
- Describe the physical activities you pursue on a regular basis outside of class. Which is your favorite, how often do you do it, and why is it your favorite?
- Pretend you want to explain to a blind friend how to throw a ball overhand. How would you describe it?
- Identify as many physical activities as you can that are offered to you in town, outside of school. If you were to participate in one, which one would it be and why?
- What three things would you have to do to improve your time in the one-mile run?
- What activities might you do to improve your muscular strength?
- Why is it important for team members to follow the game rules? What might happen if players don't follow them?

By carefully wording your questions or statements, you can get valuable feedback about your teaching, the students' feelings and concerns about what takes place in class, their general understanding of the relationships of physical activity to wellness, and how well they do or do not understand what you have presented. By having only one class write on a given day, you will not have to allot a great deal of time to read each response carefully. The communication becomes even more interactive, personal, and meaningful if you add comments about what they wrote and return the writings to the students.

The sharing of ideas and feelings could be further expanded by discussing them with the students during their next physical education class. Continue the dialogue by having the same class of students respond to more questions or statements every fourth class for a month. Once you have a fairly accurate understanding of this class's concerns, feelings, and knowledge of the activities, select another one for interaction. Do this with several classes throughout the year.

Students are generally open and honest in their responses if the climate of the class is warm and accepting. There are times, however, when you may want anonymous feedback to a question. Make it clear to the students that you are seeking a better understanding of their concerns so that you can do a better job as a teacher.

It is a good modeling technique for the teacher to write while the students do. It gives the teacher an opportunity to reflect on the question or statement presented as it relates to that class and to share those observations with the students.

Another writing technique is to use a graphic organizer for organizing thoughts and ideas before elaborating on them. An example of this technique is the "octopus." Draw an octopus on a sheet of paper and write the topic to be discussed in the head. Distribute copies of the octopus to the students. Ask the students to write on each leg of the octopus all that is important for understanding the theme or unit.

An example of this technique is shown in the figure that follows. For the game of volleyball, you might ask, "What are some of the things you must learn to play the game of volleyball effectively?" Ask the students to write the answers on the legs of the octopus. Students need not think of eight topics; they can identify more or fewer. Once they have exhausted their ideas, have the students select one topic and write all they know about it on the back of the paper.

This is a quick and easy way to gain a pretty good idea of how much your students know about a given topic. It also provides an opportunity for the students to reflect on the various elements included in the topic. Practices and drills may become more meaningful and acceptable, once students have better insight into how the various skills fit into the big picture.

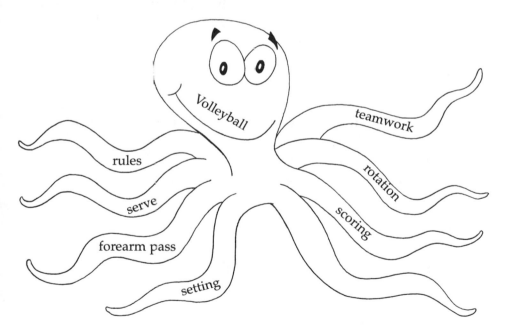

Some of the advantages of having students write include the following:

- The writing documents whether the students grasp the concepts being taught.
- It provides an opportunity for individual feedback.
- It makes you aware of individual student concerns.
- It develops organizational, thinking, and writing skills.
- It creates a journal of experiences, in which the students can better visualize their progress.
- It provides an opportunity for students to express themselves about real-life happenings.

# The Top 10

When a student was unable to participate in the physical education class, I asked her to list the top 10 reasons why students enjoy physical education. I was fascinated by her response, so I asked other students to do the same when they were unable to participate. Shown below is the result of compiling the top-10 lists of many students.

## Students' Top-10 List

10. We get to grade ourselves.
9. We are taught to make goals for ourselves and to try our hardest to achieve them.
8. We have plenty of supplies.
7. The activities are challenging.
6. Physical education relieves stress from our day.
5. We are always doing different things, so it's interesting and you never get bored.
4. Teachers are supportive, understanding, and are easy to get along with.
3. We get a good workout.
2. We are always active.
1. Teachers make physical education fun!

I also compiled a top-10 list for what I felt was important in a physical education program.

## Teacher's Top-10 List

10. Have enough equipment for each student.
9. Chart each child's progress and motivate him/her to do his/her personal best.
8. Play the game.
7. Make lessons interesting, progressive, and challenging.
6. Keep the development of self-responsibility as a top priority.
5. Develop individual and cooperative skills.
4. Provide equipment that is developmentally appropriate.
3. Present a variety of offerings so that each child can experience success.
2. Keep students physically active as much as possible.
1. Treat each child fairly and with respect.

# 6th Inning

# Monitoring Student Progress

Students who are given an opportunity to monitor their own progress in physical activities are more likely to be motivated to meet the following content standards:

1. Demonstrates competency in many movement forms and proficiency in a few movement forms.

2. Applies movement concepts and principles to the learning and development of motor skills.

7. Understands that physical activity provides opportunities for enjoyment, challenge, self-expression, and social interaction.

Formative evaluative techniques can be effective motivators and efficient monitors. When students are given the opportunity to track their own progress, they become aware of the cause and effect of their own efforts. The student can feel successful when the goal is to improve his/her own performance.

Students should feel that each time they participate in physical education, they have a reasonable chance for success. Physical education affords many opportunities to record benchmarks to use to monitor progress. A system of benchmarks can be easily managed by providing the class list on a clipboard and having the students record their own scores. In succeeding classes, the students work to improve their scores. Such records provide instant feedback that is a powerful motivator for improvement, no matter how skilled the student is.

Assessment makes students more accountable for their own learning. Middle school students need and appreciate the opportunity to be self-responsible and to have control over their learning progress. If records are kept over the three years they are in middle school, the results can be dramatic and very informative.

Following are several examples of the skills conducive to this type of student record keeping.

# Volleyball

When introducing the volleyball unit, explain to the students that they will be responsible for testing themselves on the forearm pass, the serve, and the set. They may test themselves before class begins or during a designated time during the class period. Students should write a P next to their name and the test item when they successfully complete the following test items:

## Three out of five underhand serves

**Five successive forearm passes against a wall**

**Ten successful sets with a partner**

A sample of the score sheet is shown in the form that follows. Any test item successfully completed in the sixth grade does not have to be retaken in the seventh grade. Only the specific skill or skills a student was unable to complete in sixth grade would be attempted again in the seventh and/or eighth grades.

## Volleyball, 1996–1997

| Name | Grade | Forearm pass | Serve | Set |
|------|-------|--------------|-------|-----|
| Susan | 6 | P | P | |
| John | 6 | | P | |
| Marion | 6 | P | P | P |
| Jack | 6 | P | | |
| Mija | 6 | P | P | P |
| Mary | 6 | | P | |
| Juan | 6 | P | | |
| Mike | 6 | P | P | P |
| Diane | 6 | P | P | P |
| Debbie | 6 | | P | |
| Total # | 10 | % passed 70 | 80 | 50 |

# Track-and-Field Activities

The following form shows how a spreadsheet can be used to record scores on track-and-field events.

## Track-and-field events

| Name | 50 meters | | | 100 meters | | |
|---|---|---|---|---|---|---|
| Grade | 6 | 7 | 8 | 6 | 7 | 8 |
| Josh | 8.5 | 8.3 | 7.9 | 15.5 | 14.9 | 14.0 |
| Huang | 8.7 | 8.2 | 7.7 | 15.8 | 15.0 | 13.9 |
| Natasha | 9.2 | 8.8 | 8.3 | 18.5 | 17.0 | 15.0 |
| Jose | 8.6 | 8.6 | 8.4 | 18.3 | 18.5 | 16.0 |
| Jackie | 9.0 | Med | 8.5 | 19.3 | Med | 16.8 |
| Mary | 7.9 | 7.8 | 7.6 | 15.9 | 15.5 | 14.9 |
| Joe | 8.0 | 8.0 | 7.8 | 15.0 | 14.8 | 14.8 |

| Name | High jump | | | Long jump | | |
|---|---|---|---|---|---|---|
| Grade | 6 | 7 | 8 | 6 | 7 | 8 |
| Josh | 3' 10" | 4' | 4' 4" | 10' 6" | 11' 2" | 12' 6" |
| Huang | 4' | 4' 4" | 4' 8" | 11' 0" | 11' 6" | 12' 9" |
| Natasha | 3' 10" | 4' 0" | 4' 2" | 10' 2" | 10' 8" | 11' 6" |
| Jose | 3' 8" | 3' 10" | 4' 1" | 10' 4" | 10' 8" | 11' 0" |
| Jackie | 3' 9" | Med | 4' 0" | 9' 8" | 10' 2" | 11' 0" |
| Mary | 4' 3" | 4' 5" | 4' 6" | 10' 6" | 11' 0" | 11' 9" |
| Joe | 4' 1" | 4' 1" | 4' 4" | 10' 5" | 10' 11" | 11' 5" |

# The running long jump

Have students record their best jump of the day!

# Physical Fitness Testing

The following form shows how a spreadsheet can be used to record physical fitness test items.

## Physical fitness scores

| | Pull-ups | | | Sit-ups | | |
|---|---|---|---|---|---|---|
| Grade | 6 | 7 | 8 | 6 | 7 | 8 |
| Name | | | | | | |
| Ned | 0 | 0 | 2 | 34 | 36 | 38 |
| Maria | 0 | 1 | 2 | 36 | 38 | 40 |
| Jamie | 3 | 9 | 12 | 40 | 42 | 49 |
| Chung | 2 | 4 | 9 | 41 | 42 | 45 |
| Laura | 1 | 3 | 4 | 42 | 44 | 46 |
| Richard | 0 | 1 | 2 | 34 | 36 | 38 |
| Marion | 4 | 8 | 14 | 39 | 44 | 52 |

| | Sit and reach | | | Mile run | | |
|---|---|---|---|---|---|---|
| Grade | 6 | 7 | 8 | 6 | 7 | 8 |
| Name | | | | | | |
| Ned | 25 | 27 | 31 | 10:22 | 9:34 | 9:10 |
| Maria | 27 | 28 | 32 | 9:35 | 9:15 | 8:10 |
| Jamie | 19 | 25 | 26 | 8:45 | 8:02 | 7:30 |
| Chung | 22 | 25 | 29 | 8:12 | 7:15 | 6:00 |
| Laura | 27 | 29 | 34 | 8:55 | 7:45 | 7:10 |
| Richard | 27 | 28 | 30 | 9:15 | 8:59 | 8:10 |
| Marion | 25 | 26 | 28 | 9:00 | 8:23 | 7:30 |

The results of the testing give you a good idea of which skill areas need work and which ones students have effectively learned. They also identify for you which students can benefit from additional instruction and practice.

# 7th Inning

# Debriefing

> **Debriefing can help students meet the following content standards in physical education:**
>
> 5. Demonstrates responsible personal and social behavior in physical-activity settings.
> 6. Demonstrates understanding and respect for differences among people in physical-activity settings.
> 7. Understands that physical activity provides opportunities for enjoyment, challenge, self-expression, and social interaction.

A debriefing is a group discussion or evaluation of what took place. It is a time when all students have an opportunity to express themselves. It focuses on what happened, what the outcome means, and what will be done about it.

Leading a debrief is one of the most difficult skills to learn to do well. It involves creating an atmosphere that facilitates sharing, having a sense of timing to know when and how long to debrief, and knowing what questions to ask, how to keep the focus on those issues, how to accurately interpret the verbal and nonverbal responses, and when and how to effectively bring about closure to the debrief.

When leading a debriefing it is important to focus on one issue at a time with specific goals and objectives in mind. Only ask open-ended questions that cannot be answered with a yes or no. Focus on how individuals feel about what took place. Keep the group's attention on the speaker and pay attention to what is said both verbally and non-verbally (body language). It is often helpful to summarize what was said in your own words to verify the accuracy of your understanding as well as that of the group. Be nonjudgmental and let each student be him/herself. Never allow an individual's personal worth to be attacked. Show positive energy and trust the group to draw conclusions that will improve their interactions. Be honest and sincere, and show respect for each individual. Show appreciation for the positive things students do and say. Don't hesitate to confront problems as they arise so that they may be resolved.

Put as much time and effort into planning productive interactions between students as you do preparing the rest of your lesson.

It takes a good deal of practice and experience to feel comfortable leading a debriefing session, and perhaps years to become truly proficient at it. A good way to begin to establish a climate that allows and invites sharing is to set the ground rules and model them. The ground rules may include the following:

- Focus attention on the person who is talking.
- Listen carefully to what the speaker has to say.
- Accept the feelings of others.
- Be sincere about what you share.
- Never attack an individual's personal worth.

As the leader of a debriefing session you are the facilitator in the discussion. Allow the students to do most of the talking and to draw their own conclusions. Keep the debriefing focused, simple, and short. Discuss an issue from which you want the class to learn. It could be about teamwork, effort, performance, strategy, feelings, or acceptance and compassion for others.

You can start a debriefing with an open-ended question. "Why do you think the activity went so well?" "How did you feel during the activity?" "Can you explain what happened in this activity?" It is not necessary to resolve all issues during a debriefing. The purpose is to discuss concerns and ideas as a group so the group may better understand the human interactions that took place. It is important that the students learn from one another and that you avoid pointing things out or preaching to them.

Another way to begin a debriefing is to have each participant state one word that describes his/her feelings about the activity. This technique is often referred to as a "whip." Once you have a sense of the class's feelings, end the session by summarizing them in a few words. If the group was very positive about the experience, you might say, "You enjoyed it!" "What made it work so well!" "What do you feel most proud of?" End with a remark such as, "You showed a lot of good team work and effort today. Keep it up." If the group expressed negative feelings, you might say, "Many of you were frustrated." "Can you explain why you felt that way?" "What did you learn about yourself?" "What did you learn about others?" What changes should we make to make the class work better?" End the debriefing by stating the changes you will make based on their suggestions. Add, "Let's see if that improves the class!"

Another quick way to get student feedback is to use the thumbs-up signal. A thumbs-up means you approve of what took place. It was satisfying and successful. A thumbs-down means you were dissatisfied, frustrated, or you disliked the activity. A thumb placed horizontally indicates the activity was OK but could be improved. This expeditious visual evaluation may be all the information you need at times, or it may be a quick way to initiate a discussion about why students feel the way they do.

## The debriefing process

---

| | |
|---|---|
| 1. Ask open-ended questions. | • What happened?<br>• How did you feel about that? |
| 2. Verify perceptions. | • Summarize the responses as you understood them.<br>• Is that correct? |

3. Make connections.

- Did anyone feel differently?
- What can we learn from that?
- What changes do you think we should make?
- What similar experiences have you had elsewhere? How were the problems resolved?
- Does anyone have any other suggestions?

4. Make changes.

- Let's try what you suggested to see how it works!

5. Evaluate changes.

- Are you happy with the changes?
- Is there anything you would like to add?

6. Closure.

- You came up with some excellent ideas. We will see how well they work in the next class.

If leading a debriefing session is a new skill you are learning, begin slowly. Don't dive right in. Learn bit by bit so you don't end up drowning. What students can learn from well-run debriefs is well worth the time and effort it takes to learn the art of debriefing.

Debriefs give students the opportunity to reflect on and analyze their group experience so that they may better understand their personal and group interactions. They provide a safe setting for students to express their feelings and better understand the feelings of others. Over time the students may develop more mature ways to think and behave. They may become more compassionate, respectful, accepting of differences, cooperative, and better able to relate to others. Debriefing sessions can be effective ways to enhance group spirit. They may help to build self-confidence and self-esteem.

**Go for it!**

# References

*The art and science of processing experiences.* Clifford C. Knapp.

*The adventure wave — The structure and process of adventure experience.* Nicki Hall, Karl Rohnke, and Steve Butler.

Both publications can be obtained from

Project Adventure
P.O. Box 100
Hamilton, MA 01936

# 8th Inning

# Parent Involvement

> "We all wound up the evening knowing each other better. We were challenged to do our best; we worked hard and had some humorous moments. Most of all we learned to demand more of ourselves and how to work together to help one another accomplish our goal. We ended the evening totally exhilarated."
> —Bill Oppenheimer, parent of a former sixth grade student

Involve parents in their child's physical education. Don't assume your students are telling them what they have accomplished in physical education. Most don't! At the same time, parents are generally preoccupied with many other things in their lives and give little thought to what their child is experiencing in physical education. Also, many parents don't have fond memories of their physical education experiences. When asked about their experiences, parents commonly responded as follows:

"We were involved in single-sex programs."

"I was picked at the end because my skills were not very good."

"It was extremely competitive and I was too shy to enjoy it."

"We played far too many bombardment-type games."

"Too many times, the gym teacher would just 'roll the ball out' and the athletes got to play most of the time."

"I always felt like a 'klutz'; that I couldn't do anything well."

With a program that promotes cooperation and caring as well as competition, you have an opportunity to demonstrate to parents the value and joy of physical activities in a way they may have never experienced. Cooperative games, initiatives, international games, and activities such as those described in Game #2, 5th Inning, work especially well for parents' nights to which students are also invited.

# Parents' Night

Since sixth graders are just entering middle school and many of their parents are becoming acquainted with it for the first time, inviting students and parents to a parents' night is a very enjoyable and effective way to acquaint parents with your program. Invite only one class and their parents at a time, to maximize your interactions with them. Various classes may be invited periodically throughout the year. Plan activities that can be effectively done with the students and parents working together. Cooperative games and initiatives are especially appropriate. These activities require cooperation, problem solving, and exuberant physical activity—plus, they are a lot of fun! Also, many of these activities are ones most parents have never experienced during their own schooling. The purpose of the evening is to allow parents to experience the joy of the physical activities that promote your program goals, to help parents better understand the value of the activities presented, and to gain parent support for your program. If well planned and executed, parents' night can be a very effective tool for promoting physical education.

Begin the evening with activities that actively involve all the parents and students. Examples of these activities follow.

**Pairs Tag:** Place four Kontrol Kones to mark a square approximately 20 feet x 20 feet (for about 30 players). Find someone you don't know to be your partner. Decide which partner will initially be It. Those who are It will try to tag their chosen partner, who, of course, will attempt to keep from being tagged. You must stay within the square designated by the four cones. Only fast walking is allowed—no running! If you tag your partner, switch positions. The new It must stand still for three seconds before pursuing his/her partner. Begin when the music starts. Having many pairs pursuing one another at the same time in a restricted area is what makes the game interesting and fun.

Have the group begin when the music starts and stop when the music stops. Find a new partner and repeat the activity.

**Triangle Tag:** Get into groups of four—two parents and two students in each group. Spread the groups out away from one another. Three people in each group hold hands to form a triangle. The fourth person is It. If you're It, select the person in the triangle you wish to tag. Hand-holders try to block the It and protect the one selected to be tagged, as you count to seven. After the seven-second count or a successful tag is made, one of the people forming the triangle becomes the new It. Allow all participants to have a turn being It.

Other good activities for a parent's night include: Frog It, Frogs and Flies, and Assembly Line. (See Game #2, 5th Inning for descriptions of these activities.) Still more activities can be found in the books written by Karl Rohnke. His publications are available through Project Adventure, Inc. The address can be found in the resource section at the end of this book.

The next segment of the parents' night may include group problem-solving initiatives such as: Entanglement (see Game #2, 5th Inning), Rolling River Raft (see Game #2, 5th Inning), and Nuclear Waste Transfer (described below)

**Nuclear Waste Transfer:** (original idea from Phillip E. Gerney) This activity requires an octagonal piece of wood with holes drilled through it. Four strings are strung through the holes to make eight ends. On top of the octagon is a plastic foam cylinder that is weighted at the bottom. The octagon is placed on a platform or inside a hoop. The group must work cooperatively to move the nuclear waste from one platform or hoop to another, about 25 feet away, without having it fall. If the nuclear waste does fall, the activity is tried again from the beginning.

The Rolling River Raft activity takes more time and more participants than entanglement and nuclear waste transfer. Involve half of the group in the Rolling River Raft, while the other half does both Entanglement and Nuclear Waste Transfer. The participants in the Entanglement and Nuclear Waste Transfer activities exchange after completing the activity they started with. You may need two Nuclear Waste Transfer stations, depending on the size of the group. These activities are only examples. Many of the activities described in the 5th Inning can also be presented.

Once everyone has participated in the warm-up and initiative activities, bring the group together for a debriefing session. Begin by asking, "Parents, do you remember doing any activities similar to the ones you just participated in when you were in school?" "Share with us some of your physical education experiences." "Students, what would you like to tell your parents about your physical education experiences?" "What have you learned about yourself in your physical education classes?" "How would you describe the experience you had tonight at parent's night?"

Our parents' nights conclude with the students helping their parents put on their studebaker wraps (rope climbing harnesses) in preparation for their climb on one of the three indoor climbing walls. If time permits, students are given the opportunity to climb the walls as well. For most parents, climbing a wall is a new experience. It can be a challenging, frightening, exhilarating, and a very positive experience for them. Sharing such an experience with their child makes it a very unique and unforgettable evening for parents.

If adventure programming is not part of your school curriculum, other activities such as international games, volleyball, and other activities such as those described in Game #2, 5th Inning may be used. Our parents' nights programs are very well received and do more to promote our physical education program than anything else I ever did in my 35 years of teaching physical education.

# Open House

Most schools have an open house in the fall, when all parents are invited to attend their child's classes and meet the teachers. An open house is a wonderful public-relations opportunity for you to promote your program. A pamphlet, like the one that follows, could be handed out and discussed. Emphasize your main goals and objectives and state how students will be graded. Briefly outline some of the activities that you will teach, and don't forget to mention the upcoming parents' nights to the sixth-grade parents.

## Student and Parent Mile Run

When you teach a unit on cross-country, invite the parents to walk or run the mile with their child's class.

Another way you can involve parents is to have them participate in a school-wide run during or after school. If you make this an annual event, you could record each participant's time. The challenge would be to see how much you could improve your time the following year. The emphasis would be not on who ran the fastest, but who improved the most.

## The Pamphlet

Send a pamphlet explaining your physical education program in the school's summer mailing, or hand it out during the fall open house. Include an explanation about how students will grade themselves based on criteria the students helped formulate. A sample pamphlet is shown on pages 75-76.

When report cards are sent home, include each student's physical fitness score as well as his/her grade. You may also include suggestions about how parents can help their child improve his/her physical fitness. Your suggestions could be presented to all parents or they may be individualized prescriptions for a specific student. Inform your students about what you are including.

Learning should be a lifelong journey. Students and parents working together are more likely to make that journey a positive and rewarding one.

## Welcome to the John Read Middle School Physical Education Program

A   B   C   D

## The Difference Between Ordinary and Extra Ordinary is that Little *Extra!*

## Physical Education Activities

- Learn team games using the grid system
- Play team handball, school rugby, soccer, lacrosse, and ultimate keep-away games
- Set personal physical fitness benchmarks
- Run in a cross-country meet
- Learn the skills and play:
  - basketball
  - volleyball
  - floor hockey
- Learn about the link between physical activity and a healthy life style
- Participate in striking skill activities such as:
  - tennis
  - golf
  - badminton
  - softball
  - rounders
  - cricket
- Learn basic tumbling skills
- Learn to move to music:
  - sports skills done to music
  - line dancing
  - folk and square dancing
- Assess one's knowledge and skill level in physical education by:
  - writing
  - taking skill tests
- Participate in circus art skills
- Test yourself in track and field activities

## Project Adventure Program

- New games
- Initiatives
- Indoor ropes course
  - wall climbing, etc.
  - indoor trapeze
  - indoor zip line
- Outdoor low ropes course
  - trust fall
  - hickory jump
  - tire and the pole
  - tension traverse
  - TP shuffle
- Outdoor high ropes
  - heebe jee bee
  - trapeze jump
  - two line bridge
  - cat walk
  - zip line
  - vertical playpen
  - rappelling station
  - dangle duo
  - centipede
- Rock climbing

## Some Thoughts to Keep in Mind

- Be on time! If you need to see a teacher or work on a project, you MUST see Mrs. Bowen or Mr. Hichwa first and obtain permission.
- You are responsible for yourself! Stretch properly and participate to the best of your ability. It is your life and health we are trying to improve — realize it! Make no excuses - JUST DO IT!
- WORK HARD - LEARN TO PLAY TOGETHER - SET GOALS

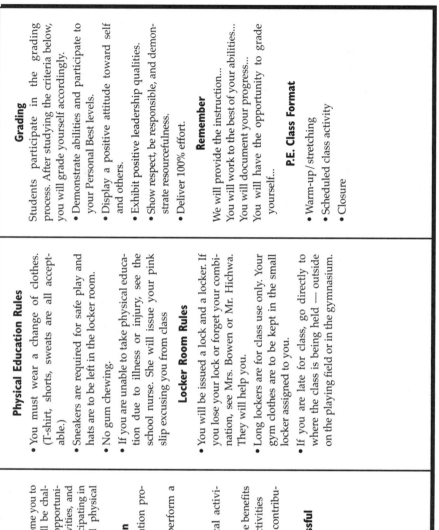

## Welcome

Mrs. Bowen and Mr. Hichwa welcome you to physical education where you will be challenged, treated fairly, have many opportunities to partake in a variety of activities, and have fun doing it! You will be participating in a health, Project Adventure, and physical education class every day.

## JRMS Physical Education

The goals of the physical education program are as follows:

- Learn the skills necessary to perform a variety of physical activities
- Become physically fit
- Participate regularly in physical activities both in and out of school
- Know the implications of and the benefits from involvement in physical activities
- Value physical activity and its contribution to a healthful lifestyle

## Guidelines for your Successful Participation

- Dress daily
- Follow directions
- Listen carefully
- Give your maximum effort

## Physical Education Rules

- You must wear a change of clothes. (T-shirt, shorts, sweats are all acceptable.)
- Sneakers are required for safe play and hats are to be left in the locker room.
- No gum chewing.
- If you are unable to take physical education due to illness or injury, see the school nurse. She will issue your pink slip excusing you from class

## Locker Room Rules

- You will be issued a lock and a locker. If you lose your lock or forget your combination, see Mrs. Bowen or Mr. Hichwa. They will help you.
- Long lockers are for class use only. Your gym clothes are to be kept in the small locker assigned to you.
- If you are late for class, go directly to where the class is being held — outside on the playing field or in the gymnasium.

## Grading

Students participate in the grading process. After studying the criteria below, you will grade yourself accordingly.

- Demonstrate abilities and participate to your Personal Best levels.
- Display a positive attitude toward self and others.
- Exhibit positive leadership qualities.
- Show respect, be responsible, and demonstrate resourcefulness.
- Deliver 100% effort.

## Remember

We will provide the instruction...
You will work to the best of your abilities...
You will document your progress...
You will have the opportunity to grade yourself...

## P.E. Class Format

- Warm-up/stretching
- Scheduled class activity
- Closure

# 9th Inning

# The E + I + P = A Theory

> "Success is a journey, not a destination."
> —Ben Sweetland

What makes a program successful? What are the critical components that get students motivated to quickly change their clothes, play, and work enthusiastically and cooperatively with their peers?

To me the following equation defines success in physical education:

Effort + Instruction + Progress = Achievement

The gifted athlete views success differently than the physically-challenged student—the "right fielder." How can the instructor make it possible for each student, regardless of his/her athletic ability, to achieve success? I believe that is possible only when both the teacher and the students put in the effort, the instruction is appropriate, challenging, and fun, and the students are aware of their progress.

# Effort

Effort directly correlates to the quality of the environment and the instruction. Students will respond with enthusiasm when the class is nonthreatening, challenging, and well-presented.

# + Instruction

Achievement is directly related to the quality of the instruction. The quality of instruction is based on the ability of the teacher to relate to each student, as well as his knowledge and skill at presenting the subject matter.

# + Progress

One of the greatest motivators is being aware that improvement or progress is taking place. When students chart their own progress, success is guaranteed if effort is put into it.

# = Achievement

Students feel a sense of accomplishment or achievement when their efforts come from within. That is possible for most students only in an environment that is open, nonthreatening, inclusive, well-organized, challenging, and fun. Students must be treated with respect, encouraged to be self-responsible, and given opportunities to express themselves.

My goal is for the students to feel at ease with one another and to be encouraged and invigorated by one another. With well-planned instruction that challenges and encourages them, students will make progress in working toward their personal best. Their accomplishments make them feel successful, a feeling that may be expressed as achievement.

When students are asked to assess themselves, they can look at the figure that follows and at the shadow as a reflection of themselves and decide just what they have achieved. If they have met the grading criteria outlined in Game #1, 5th Inning, they can give themselves an A.

# PLAY BALL

# GAME #2

**A series of activities
toward a more inclusive
physical education program for the
middle school student**

# 1st Inning

# Effective Warm-Ups

> **By making warm-ups interesting, varied, challenging, and fun, you will help students meet the following content standards:**
>
> 3. Exhibits a physically active lifestyle.
> 4. Achieves and maintains a health-enhancing level of physical fitness.
> 7. Understands that physical activity provides the opportunity for enjoyment, challenge, self-expression, and social interaction.

"The most significant reason for students to continue to exercise is if they have fun in those activities."

—Karl Rohnke

No truer words have ever been spoken. The traditional warm-up exercises of jumping jacks, sit-ups, push-ups, running two laps, and similar exercises can become very *boring*. If they are done frequently, students may develop a negative attitude toward physical activities in general. We need to make the warm-up phase of the physical education class interesting, meaningful, challenging, and fun. But how?

Vary the warm-up exercises and, whenever possible, relate them to the main activity for that class. Students are quick to point out their likes and dislikes. If they don't see the connection or value of the activity, they are likely to lose interest in it.

The following activities not only get the blood flowing but set the stage for successful participation in a variety of individual and team sport activities.

## Space Movers

**Related activities:** any keep-away game or any team-sport game

Have the students spread out as far away from one another and any boundaries as possible. When the music starts, the students move under control and remain as far away from one another as they can. When the music stops, they freeze. Check to see if any large open spaces or crowded areas exist. Inform the students that every game is a space game and that moving effectively and efficiently in the space provided is an important skill to learn.

Repeat the activity, having the students move in different directions—forward, backward, sideways, upward, downward, straight, zigzag, circular, and curved; at different levels—high, medium, and low; and at varying speeds—slow, moderate, and fast.

# The Moving Wall

**Related activities:** any game involving space limitations

Have the students move under control in a designated area, staying as far away from one another as possible. On a signal, students stop. Make the space smaller and repeat the activity. Each time the students stop, the area is made smaller. Discuss what effect the size of the area had on their movements.

## Back-to-Back

**Related activities:** activities that require trust and cooperation

Students stand back-to-back with a partner. On a designated signal, partners walk away from one another. On a second signal, partners return to the back-to-back position. Other movements that can be used are jogging, running, skipping, and walking. Try the activity with eyes closed.

# Jumping Rope, Make Believe

**Related activities:** all running activities and team-sports

Ask the students to pick out a rope that is just right for them—one that, when doubled, comes up to their armpits. Since the rope is imaginary, it is magical. When the music starts, the students begin jumping their rope. Begin by initiating some basic rope-jumping skills that the students mimic. Once they understand the activitiy, students can demonstrate their own jump rope skills for the class to try.

Another option is to have the students pair up and take turns mimicing each other. Also try having the students work in threes, with two pretending to turn, while a third jumps. This may also be done as double Dutch.

The session can end by having the students go for a "school record"! Have the students see how many times they can turn their own rope on one jump—two? three? four? a world-record number?

This activity is a great work-out and warm-up in which everyone succeeds and no one ever misses! Do it to music. "Celebration" by Cool and the Gang works well!

## Success and Try Again

**Related activities:** any tag game or such team-sports as school rugby, basketball, or soccer

Write "SUCCESS" on one placard and "TRY AGAIN" on another. Place the placards approximately 30 to 50 feet apart. Have the students find a partner and face one another. Each student tries to touch the back of their partner's knee with the fingertips of one hand. The student who succeeds goes to the SUCCESS sign and finds another partner. The student who comes in second goes to the TRY AGAIN sign and tries again with a new partner. This continues until the teacher signals the end of the activitiy.

This is a great way to practice the basic defensive position.

What other activities can you think of that can fit into the success-and-try-again format? The following are two suggestions.

**Hunker Howser:** Student partners stand on dome multimarkers, facing each other, and approximately 10 feet apart. Each holds the end of a 12- to 15-foot rope, and attempts to pull the other off balance. The winner goes to the SUCCESS side to find a new opponent and the student who came in second finds another opponent on the TRY AGAIN side.

**One-on-One Soccer:** Pairs of students share a soccer-type ball and stand between two small cones placed approximately 10 yards apart. The students try to knock down the cone that their partners are defending.

Players who knock down their opponent's cone go to the SUCCESS side to find a new partner and those who come in second go to the TRY AGAIN side for a new partner. The ball remains at the station.

**SUCCESS Side**

**TRY AGAIN Side**

"Success and Try Again" and "Jump Flags" are the creations of John Smith, NASPE's 1989 Elementary School Teacher of the Year. I have used these two activities with great success, and the students get a great warm-up and at the same time are learning basic skills.

## Jump Flags

**Related activities:** any game that requires jumping, such as basketball or volleyball

Middle school students often jump up to touch the basketball backboard or net, the exit signs, a door frame, a point on a wall, ceiling tiles, or just about anything else that offers them a challenge. In fact, students of all ages love to test their jumping abilities. This innate desire to see how high you can jump should be encouraged. There are ways students can be challenged and find success regardless of their jumping ability.

John Smith's ingenious Jump Flags can provide such a challenge. The Jump Flags consist of a 30-foot band which is hung on an incline (at about a 20-degree angle), between two poles or a pole and wall. The angle of the band and height of the flags may be adjusted according to the ability of the students.

Students look at the height of each flag and choose to start at the one that they feel they are likely to find success at. As students improve their jumping technique and ability, they move to the next higher flag.

Using the Jump Flags, teach the jumping skills in a progressive manner. Begin with stationary jumping and progress to running one-foot take off jumps and running two-foot take-off jumps.

Place a Mini SpaceStation under each flag and a Kontrol-Kone at the beginning of each line. Have the students choose the line they would like to start at—behind the flag that is at the height they believe they can reach. Explain and demonstrate the jump you want the class to practice. Tell and show the students how they are to run around the area before getting into line to make their next jump. Remind the students that they may change lines if the flag they chose to touch is too easy or too difficult for them. Watch for the proper jumping techniques and work with those students who need help. Change the jump as the students perfect or tire of the one they are working on.

The jumping progressions follow.

## Stationary Jump Progressions

1. Use a two-foot take-off and try to touch the flag with your right hand.

2. Use a two-foot take-off and try to touch the flag with your left hand.

3. Use a two-foot take-off and try to touch the flag with both hands.

4. With your back to the flag, use a two-foot take-off and try to touch the flag with both hands behind your head.

5. With your back to the flag, use a two-foot take-off and make a half turn in the air to your left and touch the flag with your right hand.

6. With your back to the flag, use a two-foot take-off and make a half turn in the air to your left and touch the flag with your left hand.

## Running One-Foot Take-Off Progressions

1. Run and jump with a left-foot take-off, touch with the right hand.

2. Run and jump with a right-foot take-off, touch with the left hand.

3. Run and jump with a left-foot take-off, touch with two hands.

4. Run and jump with a right-foot take-off, touch with two hands.

5. Run and jump with a left-foot take-off, half turn in air to right, touch with right hand.

6. Run and jump with a right-foot take-off, half turn in air to right, touch with left hand.

7. Run and jump with a left-foot take-off, half turn in air to left, touch with two hands.

8. Run and jump with a right-foot take-off, half turn in air to right, touch with two hands.

## Running Two-Foot Take-Off Progressions

1. Run and jump with a two-foot take-off, touch with right hand.

2. Run and jump with a two-foot take-off, touch with left hand.

3. Run and jump with a two-foot take-off, touch with two hands.

4. Run and jump with a two-foot take-off, half turn to left, touch with right hand.

5. Run and jump with a two-foot take-off, half turn to right, touch with left hand.

6. Run and jump with a two-foot take-off, half turn to right, two-hand touch.

7. Run and jump with a two-foot take-off, half turn to left, two-hand touch.

8. Run and jump with a two-foot take-off, two-hand touch on back of flags, behind back.

Adapted, by permission, from Sportime International, Item #171781 Jump Flag Guide.

## Sports Skill Movements to Music

**Related activities:** basketball, striking activities, or any skill you wish to include in your routine

Various sport skills may be incorporated into a movement routine and set to music. The first example that follows incorporates basic basketball skills, while the second emphasizes striking skills.

### Basketball Line Dance: Setting some basic moves to music

**Karrioka Steps**

Eight steps to the right (clap!)

Eight steps to the left (clap!)

Repeat

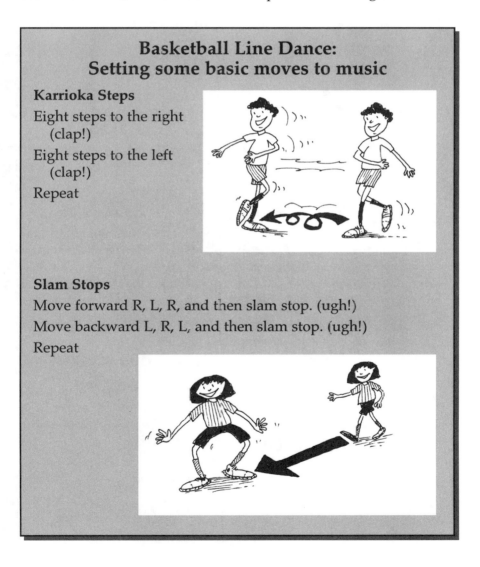

**Slam Stops**

Move forward R, L, R, and then slam stop. (ugh!)

Move backward L, R, L, and then slam stop. (ugh!)

Repeat

## Lay-Up Shooting

Go forward L, R, L and simulate a layup in basketball. (swoosh!)

Go backward R, L, R and simulate a layup with the opposite hand. (swoosh!)

Repeat

## Moving

Take eight steps forward (in various directions—not in a straight line).

Move eight steps backward (in various directions).

Repeat

# Tennis Line Dance:
## Setting some basic moves to music

**Karrioka Steps**

Eight steps to the right (clap!)

Eight steps to the left (clap!)

Repeat

**Slam Stops**

Move forward R, L, R, and then slam stop. (ugh!)

Move backward L, R, L, and then slam stop. (ugh!)

Repeat

**Ground Strokes**

Slide to the right, R, L, R, and make a 1/4 turn R while you simulate making a forehand stroke.

Slide to the left, L, R, L, and make a 1/4 turn L while you simulate making a backhand stroke.

Repeat

**Box Step**

Move forward R, L, R, and then slam stop. (ugh!)

Slide to the right two times. (clap!)

Move backward L, R, L, and then slam stop. (ugh!)

Slide to the left two times. (clap!)

Repeat

**Recommended Music**

Jock Rock Album, "Rock and Roll, Part 2"

"The Hey Song," by Gary Glitter

"Mony, Mony," by Tommy James and the Shandells

Jock Jam Album, "Get Ready 4 This," by 2 Unlimited

For that matter, any line dance can be an effective warm-up activity. It does get the blood flowing, and it's fun!

# The Infinite Relay Race

**Related activities:** all running activities

Divide the class into groups of three. Position them in rows of three as shown in the illustration that follows.

The first person in each line begins running in a clockwise direction until he/she gets back to the home position. Immediately, the next person begins running. This continues until everyone has completed two turns.

Anaerobic conditioning is a combination of exercise and rest. The above routine provides anaerobic conditioning by alternating exercising and resting. The heart rate goes up while running and down while resting.

By dribbling a basketball or soccer ball, moving in different directions, using various locomotor movements, and making the rectangle different sizes, you can make this an ideal warm-up activity for many sports.

# 2nd Inning

# Upper-Arm-Strength Activities

**Upper arm activities can help students meet the following content standards:**

2. Applies movement concepts and principles to the learning and development of motor skills.
3. Exhibits a physically active lifestyle.
4. Achieves and maintains a health-enhancing level of physical fitness.

Improving the upper-arm strength of today's youth is one of our biggest challenges. Pull-ups, or some variation of them, keep emerging on our physical fitness tests, so they must have some fitness value. The traditional activities of rope climbing, chin-ups, and push-ups have not been very successful in motivating students. So what can be done to improve the upper arm strength of today's youth?

First, establish a benchmark for each student. If a student cannot successfully perform a pull-up, then provide another activity in which the student can attain a benchmark. Push-ups done in creative ways can be a viable alternative!

The following activities take the boredom out of doing push-ups and place them in the "fun" category. Some are done individually, but most are done in tandem or in groups, so that the activity becomes a cooperative venture. Progress will more likely take place when the activity is fun, the students are working in teams, and everyone achieves a score: No one records a 0 next to his or her name.

Whether you have the students work individually or in pairs, have them establish benchmarks when doing the activities described below. Feedback is a great motivational tool. Having the students attempt to break their own best record takes some of the drudgery away. You will be pleasantly surprised at the results.

One of the keys to successful programming is to vary how students interact with one another. Have the students work on their own for a few days, then with a partner, and finally in small groups. Record keeping can be accomplished in a variety of ways. Students can record their results on a clipboard that is in the middle of the gym or field, on a large sheet of paper on a wall, or in their individual journals (portfolios). Don't forget, the students need to take responsibility for their *own* physical well being. Keeping personal records is one way to help students become more self-responsible. The *teacher* cannot do everything! Delegate some of the bookkeeping responsibilities to the students. In doing so, everyone benefits!

Students should be encouraged to do push-ups by holding their upper bodies up with their arms and their toes. For those students who are unable to hold regular push-up position they may support their lower body with their knees. If they choose the latter position (modified push-up position), they must keep their weight forward enough to give their arms a good workout.

Following are some suggestions for improving upper-arm strength.

## Individual Activities

### The Elevator

Using either the regular or the modified push-up position, begin with the students resting comfortably on the floor. You are the elevator operator. You begin by saying, "Going up." The students push-up approximately three inches off the floor and hold that position as you describe what is for sale on floor one. Or, you can point out one positive, healthy reason for having adequate upper-arm strength instead. For example, you could say, "It gives us the ability to throw and strike a ball so much farther and more accurately."

"Going up to the second," you say. The students hold a position a few more inches off the ground, while you describe the items for sale on the second floor or give another reason for developing upper-arm strength. Continue this process for four floors, and then repeat the process going down. The students hold for a short count while you briefly explain a positive reason for working on the upper-shoulder girdle area.

**First Floor**

**Second Floor**

**Third Floor**

**Fourth Floor**

### Shoulder Touches

Students get into a push-up position. On the word "go" (or when the music starts), they touch their right hand to their left shoulder and then their left hand to their right shoulder. Have the students count how many times they can touch a shoulder in 30 seconds. Vary the time depending on your students' ability. Thirty seconds gives a good workout.

### The Crab

Students get into a crab-walk position. They touch their right shoulder with their left hand and their left shoulder with their right hand, alternately. Have the students count how many they can do in 30 seconds.

### Push-Up Squash

Have the students place a Half-Ball below their chest. Each time they drop their chest to the floor the Half-Ball makes a squoosh. Have them count how many they can do in 30 seconds.

### Stacking Anything

Students place six objects (GameDisks, plastic cups, blocks) in front of them. They get into a push-up position and see how many times they can stack and unstack the objects in 30 seconds.

### Marching Push-Ups

Students get into a push-up or a modified push-up position with their hands on a line. When the music begins, their hands "march" to the beat, following this sequence:

right hand over the line forward
left hand over the line forward
right hand over the line backward
left hand over the line backward

This activity is very strenuous, so have students do it for only 15 to 20 seconds the first time. Keep track of how many seconds the class "marches" and increase the time each succeeding class if they can do it successfully.

### Juggling a Nugget

Students get into one of the two push-up positions with a tennis ball or a small beanbag between their hands. When the music begins, they take the ball or beanbag with their right hand and place it under their chin. Then, they use their left hand and place the ball or beanbag back on the floor. This is repeated, alternating left and right hands for 30 seconds. Students count how many times they place the ball or beanbag under their chin. Ask the class to remember how many times they did it this class and challenge them to do more in the next class.

## Activities with Partners

### Low-Fives

Students get into a push-up position, facing a partner. When the music starts, the partners give each other low-fives, right hand to partner's right hand and then left to left. Ask them to see how many times they can give one another a low-five in 30 seconds.

## High-Fives

Students get into a push-up position, facing a partner. When the music starts, they touch their partner's opposite shoulder with their hand: right hand to partner's left shoulder and then left hand to partner's right shoulder. Have them see how many they can do in 30 seconds.

## Spider Hockey

Partners face each other in a push-up position, approximately 12 feet apart. One partner tries to throw a Spider Ball or beanbag through the arms of the other, who tries to prevent it from going through. The partners continue taking turns. Have them see how many goals each of them can make.

## Musical Push-Ups

Partners face each other in a push-up position with a ball or bean-bag between them. When the music plays, they start to give each other high-fives. When the music stops, the players try to get the ball before their partner does.

*Variation:* Partners face each other. You name body parts—nose, back, head, cheek, etc.—and each player touches that body part on himself. When you say "ball," the players try to grab the ball or beanbag before their partner does!

## Moving Those Nuggets

Working in pairs, one student is in a push-up position and the other is standing behind his/her feet. The standing partners roll a ball on the ground to the right of their partners, who catch it with their right hands, transfer it to their left hands, and roll it back to their partners. Continue this sequence for 30 seconds, counting the number of times the ball completes the circuit. After a ten-second break, partners exchange places and repeat the activity. Add the scores of both partners and record the total.

### Variation to Moving Those Nuggets

The student who is standing rolls the ball on the floor between the legs of his/her partner who is in a push-up position. (Students who can't hold a push-up position for 30 seconds, may use the modified push-up position.) That person catches the ball and throws it over his/her head to the standing partner. See how many times you can throw the ball back in 30 seconds. Change positions and repeat the activity. Add the partners' scores together and record the total.

In the next class, the partners attempt to break their own record. This activity can be repeated in the next three or four classes and again later in the year.

*Note:* Make a tape with several 30-second segments of music. Include a 10-second blank period between each 30-second music segment.

## Activities in Groups

### Around the World

Four to six students get into a push-up position and form a circle with their feet in the center and their heads facing out. The students pass a Spider Ball or beanbag from one person to the next around the circle. The group counts the number of passes they can make in 30 seconds.

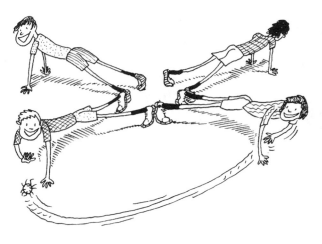

### Just Keep Doing It

Four or five students get into a row in the push-up position with their legs apart. The first person in the row passes a Spider Ball or beanbag between the arms and legs of those behind him or her. The last person in the row catches it and runs to the front of the line, beginning the process over. Count how many passes the group can complete in one minute.

## Kick It Around

Four or five students make a circle while in the crab-walk position with their heads facing in. Players on opposite sides of the circle are about 10 feet apart. Players kick the Spider Ball clockwise and count to see how many passes the group can make in 30 seconds. Do the activity again passing the Spider Ball counter clockwise and try to beat the first score.

## Pass It Around

Four or five students get into a circle in the push-up position with about 10 feet between players on opposite sides of the circle. A Spider Ball is passed from one player to another as they count to see how many passes the group can make in 30 seconds.

**Let's Play**

Team A is playing team B. A team A player attempts to pass a Spider Ball to a teammate. If a team B player successfully captures the Spider Ball, then she or he tries to pass it to a teammate. Have students just keep doing it for the fun of it!

**Dyna-Bands**

This activity is an exercise program choreographed to music using short pieces of latex bands (Dyna-Bands). The students will improve their muscular strength and endu-rance and have fun doing it! The band is stretched to the side, up and down, behind the head, etc. to a specified number of beats. You lead the class and the stretches are made in unison.

Two choreographed routines are described below. Use them only as examples. Students love to create, and this activity offers a perfect opportunity for them to design their own Dyna-Band routine.

# Meet the Flintstones

Performed by the B 52's

**Introduction:** Quick short horizontal pulls for a warm-up

**Verse 1**

Four horizontal arm pulls in front of body

Four overhead horizontal arm pulls

Eight alternating right and left "heart pulls" (one hand on chest with the other arm pulling to the side)

Six pulls with left arm held straight out in front and the right hand pulling the band in a downward direction

Six pulls with the right arm held straight out in front and the left hand pulling the band down

Have the students rest for a moment while they position the Dyna-Band behind their back and across their shoulder blades.

**Verse 2**

Eight pulls, alternating right and left, pressing arms forward

Eight pulls, alternating right and left, pressing arms to the side

Eight pulls, alternating right and left, pressing arms forward

Eight pulls, alternating right and left, pressing arms to the side

Four pulls, alternating right and left, pressing arms forward

Four pulls, alternating right and left, pressing arms to the side

**Verse 3**

Repeat verse one

**Finish:** Short quick horizontal arm pulls with full extension for the ending

# Addam's Family Dyna-Band Routine

Movie Soundtrack produced by Joe Reismann

**Chorus:**

2 quick front horizontal pulls—pause
2 quick front horizontal pulls—longer pause
2 quick front horizontal pulls—pause
2 quick front horizontal pulls—pause
2 quick front horizontal pulls—longer pause
2 quick front horizontal pulls

**Section 1:** Eight long slow front horizontal pulls. Hold band at center of chest, shoulder high, and stretch both arms out to sides.
Repeat chorus

**Section 2:** Four overhead pulls. Hold bands with arms overhead and pull out and down to shoulders.
Repeat chorus

**Section 3:** Eight side pulls. Hold band with hands down in front of body. Pull outward and up to shoulder height.
Repeat chorus

**Section 4:** Eight alternating right and left "heart pulls"—both hands on center of chest. Alternately, stretch right arm straight out to the right. Return to chest. Take left arm out to left and return. Repeat eight times.
Repeat chorus

**Section 5:** Double time short front pulls. (See how many you can do.)
Repeat chorus

**Section 6:** Four simulated tennis backhands. Begin with both hands at left thigh and stretch right arm forward (like hitting a tennis backhand). Return to thigh and repeat.

Four simulated tennis backhands—left handed player. Begin with both hands at right thigh and stretch left arm forward.
Repeat chorus

**Section 7:** Finish with four front pulls and hold one long pull until the end of the music.

I want to thank John Smith for sharing this wonderful "Adams Family" Dyna-Band routine.

# Dueling Banjos: A Dyna-Band Routine

Produced by Warner Bros., performed by Eric Weissberg.

This routine does not have a pattern to it. It is meant to be creative. You can be the leader and have the class mirror your movements, or you can divide the class in half and have one group lead the other.

*Please note:* Work the muscles throughout the full range of motion. Don't hyperextend or lock the joints.

# 3rd Inning

# Keep-Away Activities

Being actively involved in the keep-away activities described in this inning can lead to the fulfillment of the following content standards:

1. Demonstrates competency in many movement forms and proficiency in a few movement forms.

2. Applies movement concepts and principles to the learning and development of motor skills.

3. Exhibits a physically active lifestyle.

4. Achieves and maintains a health-enhancing level of physical fitness.

5. Demonstrates responsible personal and social behavior in physical-activity settings.

7. Understands that physical activity provides opportunities for enjoyment, challenge, self-expression, and social interaction.

Every game is a space game. Learning to move with or without a ball, between lines, and among teammates and opponents are skills that are basic to the understanding of and successful execution in most team games. Keep-away activities teach students basic movement strategies. They will then be more knowledgeable—and thus more successful—when they play such team games as basketball, soccer, lacrosse, team handball, touch football, school rugby, and field hockey.

## Lead-Up Activities to Playing Keep-Away

Each student should have his or her own ball to dribble, throw, catch, kick, shoot, and juggle. Begin by having the students experience a variety of ways of using their ball while staying in their personal space. Next, have the students move and make their ball do something, with emphasis on ball control in general space. *General space* is defined as the entire space available for play in which everyone can move, and *personal space* is only the space surrounding the individual.

**Personal space— the area within the student's reach**

## General space—
## the area that is open, not occupied
## by another person

### With Partners

1. Two students throw an object to each other. The distance between them is relatively short. The receiver "rattles" his or her fingers at chest height for a target. Check for the most efficient throwing method. As students become more proficient in throwing and catching, have them increase the distance between them.

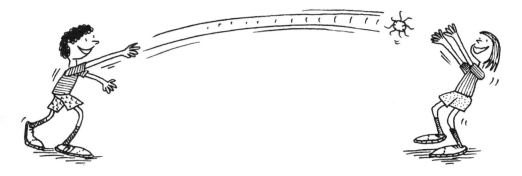

2. One partner, who is stationary, throws an object to a moving target, the other partner.

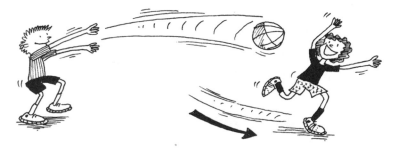

3. A student throws an object to her or his partner while moving to the right or left. The receiver remains stationary, moving only to receive the ball.

4. One partner throws on the run to a moving partner.

5. A student throws to a partner who fakes one way and then goes the other way.

6. The "Willie Mays Catch": A student throws to a partner on the run, who catches it over the shoulder, going away!

7. The Long Pass: A student throws the ball as far as he or she can toward a partner, who catches it on the run.

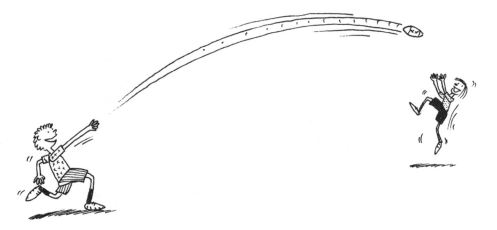

## With Teams

1. Two-on-One: Two students attempt to keep an object away from a third student. When the defender catches or touches the object, the thrower becomes the defender.

2. Two-on-Two: Two students attempt to keep an object away from two other students. The goal is to complete as many passes as possible before the other team can intercept or touch the object being thrown.

3. Three-on-Two: This activity is the same as two-on-two, except that the offensive team (the team with the ball) has three members, and the object may not be thrown to the same team member more than two consecutive times. When the defense gains possession, the thrower joins them on the new offensive team.

4. Three-on-Three: Each team makes as many consecutive passes as possible before the object is intercepted. The object may not be thrown to the same team member more than two consecutive times.

5. Ultimate Keep-Away, Three-on-Three: Each team has a goal line at one end of the playing area. Team members pass the object to one another and score a point when a teammate receives it while standing over the opponent's goal line. The opponents take possession of the object when they intercept it, it is dropped, or a point is scored.

# General Rules for Keep-Away:

1. No body contact allowed.
2. The receiver of a pass may take three steps.
3. There is a change of possession whenever the object touches the ground, the other team intercepts, or a point is scored.
4. The defender can guard his/her opponent. If the offensive person has not taken three steps, she/he may move, but the defender may not. If the offensive person has taken three steps, the defender may stay on the offensive player.

# Throwing Objects for Keep-Away

Have a bag full of objects that can be thrown and caught with ease. Let the students choose the object they would like to use. Some suggested keep-away playing implements are

rubber chickens

Frisbees

Spider Balls

rugby balls

junior-sized footballs and basketballs

small foam balls

team handballs

six-inch All-Balls

# 4th Inning

# Teaching Children How to Play Team Games Through the Grid System

> **Playing games using the grid system will help students meet the following content standards:**
>
> 1. Demonstrates competency in many movement forms and proficiency in a few movement forms.
> 2. Applies movement concepts and principles to the learning and development of motor skills.
> 3. Exhibits a physically active lifestyle.
> 4. Achieves and maintains a health-enhancing level of physical fitness.
> 5. Demonstrates responsible personal and social behavior in physical-activity settings.

Students need to learn how to play within boundaries, recognizing just how much space they have in which to play. By providing the structure, a grid, the students can practice their individual and team sport skills in pairs and small groups. By setting up several grids, you maximize participation, so that every student has the opportunity to be actively involved. By having each group in a designated area, you minimize the possibility of student collisions that may result in injury.

Small cones are recommended for outdoor play, whereas small square Mini Space Stations work well in the gymnasium. The size of the grids can vary, with the students determining the size that fits them best. Having small groups learn basic skills and drills within a designated area will maximize participation and allow the teaching of skills in a progressive manner.

# Movement Activities Within the Grid

Two people occupy a grid; size is determined by the players or teacher.

Within this arrangement, students can do the following activities:

1. Move to open spaces, stopping and starting on a signal.
2. Move in different directions and at different speeds.
3. Move and then come to a slam stop—taking off on one foot and landing on two.
4. Move, come to a slam stop, and pivot on one foot and then the other.
5. Play tag, one-on-one, by each attempting to touch the side of the knee of the partner. This activity gets the players to model the ready or defensive position.

Objects such as small cones or Mini SpaceStations can be used to delineate the grids.

# Activities Within the Grid Using Manipulatives

Make available an assortment of objects, such as playground balls, footballs, Frisbees, rubber chickens, Spider Balls, team handballs, and basketballs (all sizes). Partners choose an object to use together. Demonstrate the proper throwing and catching techniques and check for understanding by observing the students as they practice in their grids.

The throwing and catching progressions include the following.

1. Partners throw and catch with one another in their own personal space.

2. While stationary, throw to your moving target (partner).
3. Move and throw to a stationary target.
4. Move and throw to a moving target.
5. Pass to a stationary target, move, and receive a pass (give and go).
6. Fake in one direction, then move in the opposite direction, and receive a ball from a partner.

Variations could include using a ball and simulating soccer skills or giving each student a lacrosse, floor hockey, or field hockey stick and having them practice those sport skills.

# Moving to an Open Space Within a Grid

Three players take their positions in corners of the grid (players A, B, and C in the figure that follows). Player C passes to player B, who is moving to the unoccupied corner. Then player B passes to player A, who is moving to the corner that player B just vacated. Passes are to be thrown only to the sides. No passes are permitted across the grid.

Repeat.

A variation is to add a defender to the grid. As soon as the defender touches the ball, he/she replaces the last person in the grid to touch the ball, and that person becomes the new defender.

These activities involving movement to open spaces are great for basketball, soccer, and other team sports.

# Activities Involving Three People Within the Grid

1. Two students practice the above skills with the third person playing the role of the defender.

2. Player C, who is outside the grid, attempts to pass to player A, who is being defended by player B.

# Activities Involving Four People Within the Grid

1. Two students play one-on-one within the grid and two students act as posts. The offensive player within the grid tries to score by receiving a pass from one of the post players outside the end grid line. The two post players collaborate with the offensive player by passing the ball to one another until a score is made or the ball is intercepted. The other player within the grid plays defense. Once a score is made or the defensive player retrieves the ball, the players switch roles. The post players switch with the players inside the grid often. One minute on offense or defense is a workout!

2. Make the grid larger. (Have students decide the size of their own grid.) Play two-on-two. The player with the ball tries to pass to his/her teammate and a score is made if the ball is received over the end grid line.

# Activities Involving Seven People Within the Grid

1. Two teams of three play keep-away. The goal is for one team to make 15 passes before the other team intercepts. You may add the rule that if player A receives a pass from player B, he/she must pass to player C. In the center of the grid stands a post player. Either team can pass to that player when the team is in trouble. The post player must pass the ball back to the team from which she/he receives the pass.

2. Use the same format as in #1 above, but remove the post player and play three-on-three.

3. Use the same format as in #2 above, but use the end grid lines as goals. In this variation, the grid should be a rectangle, the size of which depends on the age and skill levels of the players.

4. Use the same format as in #3 above, but add some rules. Whenever a pass is *not* completed, the ball goes over to the other team. The offensive players can take up to three running steps or dribble the ball up to three times. The defensive players can play "tight," but no body contact is permitted.

5. Use the same format as #4 above, only remove the goals. Ten passes in succession among teammates can equal a goal or a point.

## Three-on-Three With Two Post Players

1. Two teams of three play keep-away. Each team is allowed one post player, who is stationary in the middle of the grid.

2. Use the same format as in #1 above, except that when a pass is made to the post player, that player exchanges places with the passer. The post player then goes on offense, and the passer becomes the new post. The defensive player guarding the one who threw the pass to the post player now must pick up a new offensive player.

# Playing Three-on-Three

Team B attempts to score on team A by throwing a pass over the end grid line or kicking a ball through two cones. The ball must hit the ground first for the goal to be allowed. If team A successfully retrieves the ball or if team B scores, team A goes on offense against team C. If team A scores or team C retrieves the ball, then team C goes on offense against team B. Soccer, lacrosse, basketball, football, field hockey, or Frisbee skills could be incorporated into this game.

# Any-Goal Soccer Within a Grid

Set the grid so that the four corner markers are different colors or numbers. Have teams play three-on-three. You or a student in the grid calls out the number or color of one of the markers. Immediately, the teams attempt to hit that marker. Once one team is successful, another number or color is called.

# Soccer Within the Grid

Play four-on-four soccer, using small goals (2 feet high x 4 feet long) or two cones approximately 8 feet apart. The ball must hit the ground before it goes through the goal to count.

When playing actual games with goals, two modifications will increase interest and participation:

Rule #1: When a player scores, he/she switches to the other team.

Rule #2: Everyone must score before a player can score another goal.

# Other Great Activities With or Without a Grid

## A Warm-Up Drill

Set up a grid and line up three students on opposite sides. The first student in line passes or kicks the ball to the first student in the line on the other side of the grid. The kicker moves to the end of the opposite line. The receiver, in turn, passes it to the first student in the opposite line and goes to the end of that line. Throw-ins, chest passes, or bounce passes can be used in this fast-moving drill.

## The Four-Corner Drill

For this fun drill, form students into four lines, one at each corner of the grid. The first person in line A yells out the name of the first person in line B and throws him/her a chest pass. The thrower immediately follows the pass, and the receiver hands it back. Quickly, the thrower hands the ball back to the receiver and goes to the end of the line B. The student in line B with the ball yells the name of the first person in line C and throws that person a chest pass, follows the pass to receive a hand-off, and then returns the ball to the receiver and goes behind line C. The process continues the same way from line C to line D and then line D to line A. At the beginning of the drill, use one ball. Add balls to the drill as the students improve. Bounce passes can also be used. Remember to have the students call out the name of the person receiving the pass.

## The Rapid-Fire Drill

Player A has one ball in his/her hand and one on the ground. She/he passes the first ball to teammate B. Quickly player A picks up the second ball and passes it to teammate C, as player B passes the first ball back to player A. Player A now passes that ball to player D. As soon as player A lets go of the pass, player C passes his/her ball back to player A. This pattern continues for a short time. Then, on your signal, everyone moves one spot to the left, so that a new student becomes the player in the A spot. The group needs to pass the ball at the correct time, thus making this activity a very cooperative one.

## The Star Drill

Five players are in a circle with a player in the middle playing defense. The player with the ball may pass it to any player around the circle except the player on her/his immediate right or left. The defensive player attempts to intercept, touch, or deflect the pass. If he/she is successful, the player making the pass goes into the center and plays defense. The goal is for the five offensive players to make 10 successful passes in succession. When the goal is achieved, one of the offensive players goes into the middle and plays defense.

Instruct the students to make chest or bounce passes. Discourage passes over the head of the defensive player. Encourage the students to fake one way and pass the other way and to pass the ball quickly.

# 5th Inning

# "For-the-Fun-of-It" Activities

## Adventures in Problem Solving and Cooperation

**Cooperative games and problem-solving activities help students meet the following content standards:**

1. Demonstrates competency in many movement forms and proficiency in a few movement forms.
4. Achieves and maintains a health-enhancing level of physical fitness.
5. Demonstrates responsible personal and social behavior in physical-activity settings.
6. Demonstrates understanding and respect for differences among people in physical-activity settings.
7. Understands that physical activity provides opportunities for enjoyment, challenge, self-expression, and social interaction.

Challenging students to be creative thinkers, respectful listeners, willing to share, and enthusiastic participants are the goals for the activities outlined below.

Initiative games are fun to play. Students find them interesting and exciting. Initiative games are an effective tool for developing student cooperation and self-responsibility. They help students learn how to listen, follow directions, and problem solve.

# Goals of the Presentation

As a teacher, your goals in this section are to

- learn techniques that will help students improve their listening, direction-following, and group problem-solving skills;
- experience using innovative equipment;
- learn to teach activities that are noncompetitive and cooperative in nature; and
- learn debriefing skills.

# Project Adventure

Project Adventure was created in 1971 as a federally-funded program to integrate the goals and techniques of Outward Bound (a wilderness program designed to teach self-sufficiency and trust) in a school setting. The Project Adventure program has four main components—"new" or cooperative games, initiatives that require group problem solving, the low elements (done on the ground, such as spider web or trust fall), and the high elements, which require participants to be on a belay while engaging in them. To teach the low and high elements, teachers must receive special training and be certified to do so. I highly recommend a full Project Adventure program, especially at the middle school level. However, I have included only "new" games and initiatives in this book for obvious reasons. To get more information about Project Adventure, refer to the resource section at the end of this book.

# Suggestions

- When introducing a game, occasionally advise the students that there will be no questions. Students are likely to be more attentive.
- Remind the students that all activities are "challenge by choice"; in other words, the choice of participating or not participating in the activity is up to them. Take every precaution to make the environment nonthreatening and supportive.
- Get involved. Teacher involvement sparks interest!
- Use creative methods to pick groups or teams. Here are some examples: Line up students according to the month or day they were born. Group those who were born in certain months or days. Another method is to have students get a partner. Then have one in each partnership sit down. All those standing are on one team and those sitting are on another!

Let's not forget about the "fun" factor:

> "This is not a serious game . . . but having fun is serious business."

This is a favorite quote of mine from Karl Rohnke, a founding member of Project Adventure. It's his genius, creativity, and enthusiasm that inspired me 20 years ago to "go for it" and establish a "new-games" component as part of a Project Adventure program. I've been having fun ever since.

Dick Prouty, executive director of Project Adventure, explains the value of fun in this way:

> "We are designed to enjoy. When we do enjoy, we learn much more efficiently, and grow in healthier directions more naturally."

So, design fun into your activities and make it one of the goals. Students will be more receptive, interested, and enthusiastic in your program offerings.

# The Role of Debriefing in Teaching Self-Responsibility

It is important to spend time discussing what transpires in each class. A debriefing session provides the opportunity for the students and teacher to assess, analyze, and better understand what took place.

In a debrief, students have an opportunity to express their point of view, share how they felt the activity went, and make suggestions about how it could be improved. The discussion should include an analysis of student interactions as well as the activity. You are the facilitator in the discussion and the students take on the responsibility of suggesting ways to improve the activity.

Some of the fun games that require student cooperation and problem-solving are explained in the following pages.

## #1 Entanglement

**Number of players:** 8-12

**Equipment:** one 1-foot rope per participant

**Directions:** Each player holds one end of her/his own rope and the end of another player's rope. Players should not hold the rope of the person on either side of them or the rope of the person holding their rope.

**Objective:** To become untangled without letting go of your ropes!

## #2 Assembly Line

**Number of players:** 5-8

**Equipment:** five or more throwable objects, such as rubber chickens, beanbag frogs, CatchBalls, six-inch All-Balls, and playground balls

**Directions:** Players stand in a circle. One player begins by tossing an object to any player in the group. Students may not pass the object to the person on their immediate right or left. The receiver throws to anyone who has not previously caught the object. This continues until every player has caught the object. The last person returns the object to the player who started the sequence. This pattern (each person throwing to the same person she/he threw to the first time) continues as more objects are added. Add another object only after the pattern has been successfully completed with the previous number of objects.

**Objective:** For the group to successfully pass as many objects as possible in a pattern that includes all players. Continue throwing and catching for as long as possible without anyone missing.

**Suggestion:** After the first try, give the group about two minutes to discuss a strategy for being more successful, and then have them try it again.

## Variations:

- Using two basketballs and two soccer balls, have the students pass the basketballs and kick the soccer balls.
- As four different kinds of implements are being passed in a pattern, have a chicken go around the circle.
- As two or more balls are being passed in a pattern, have the group move (walk, jog, skip) in a clockwise direction. On your signal, the group reverses direction.
- Using one ball, the group moves the ball in a set pattern. On your signal, the group reverses the ball's direction. Add more balls as appropriate.
- Have the group set the pattern using one ball. After mastery, the group moves in general space, and the challenge begins. The passer seeks out the receiver, but the receiver should also be ready to receive the pass and be looking out for the passer. Using a basketball, have the students begin by passing only, and then gradually add the dribble. Using a soccer ball, the students pass the ball along the ground. Add more balls according to the group's readiness.

## #3 Tunnel It

**Number of players:** 8-12

**Equipment:** one piece of flexible tubing (approximately 20 feet long), 20-30 tennis balls, and a stop watch

**Directions:** On the word "go," students put the balls in one end of the tubing and move them through it to the other end and into a box. Time them. When they finish, give them a few minutes to discuss their strategy. Have them try to beat their first time.

**Objective:** To move the balls from one end of the tube to the other as quickly as possible and to try to improve their time on the second try.

**Variation:** Students attach two tubes by holding them together and move the balls from one end of the tube to the other. See if they can do it quicker on the second attempt.

| #4 | Frog It |
|----|---------|

**Number of players:** 8-30

**Equipment:** a beanbag frog for approximately every four players and four or more boundary cones

**Directions:** Players are scattered in an area approximately 40 feet square. One person is chosen to be "It" and tries to tag any player without a frog. Players holding a frog watch carefully to see who the "It" is chasing . If the person being chased is in trouble, someone with a frog may help prevent this person from being tagged by throwing him/her a frog.

**Objective:** For players to work together and keep one another from being tagged by "It." "It" tries to tag someone without a frog.

**Variation:** Have two people be "It" at the same time. Use rubber chickens and call it "Chicken Catchitorre."

| #5 | **Throw Up** |

**Number of players:** 6-12 or more

**Equipment:** Fun Balls, CatchBalls, rubber chickens, Spider Balls, or any other throwable objects. You will need one for every two players to begin with; then you will need additional objects, up to the number of players participating.

**Directions:** Students position themselves a few feet apart. On the word "go," students holding an object throw it up in a way that allows others in the group an opportunity to catch it. Throwers may not catch their own objects. Add one more object each time the group successfully catches them all.

**Objective:** Have the class work cooperatively to see how many objects the group can throw up at the same time and successfully catch without anyone catching their own.

## #6 Frog Frolic

Frog Frolic involves a number of innovative activities that are done using beanbag frogs and balls. Have the students think of others.

**Equipment:** beanbag frogs and 8 1/2-inch playground balls

## Catch a Frog

Form a circle of four or five students. One person is in the middle of the circle, with a frog balanced on top of a playground ball. The ball and the frog are held about head high and dropped. Someone in the circle attempts to catch the frog. Take turns dropping the ball and frog.

**Variations:**

- With partners, one partner drops the ball and frog and the other catches the frog. The students should see how many catches they can make in 30 seconds.
- Both partners have a ball and frog. They drop the ball and frog at the same time and try to catch each other's frog!

## The Great American Frog Hop

Players stand in a line with a ball and a frog. Players place their frog on the ball and hold them head high. On a signal, they drop the balls to see how far their frogs can hop forward.

**Variation:** Students stand with their frogs on their ball held in front of them. The students drop their balls to make their frogs hop forward. The students repeat dropping the ball and frog from where the frog lands until the frog reaches the other side of the gymnasium.

## Frog in a Pond

Place hoops around the gym and have the students stand 8 to 10 feet away from the "pond" their frog is to hop into. Place the frog on the ball and drop it. How many ponds can your frog hop into?

**Variation:** Place a hoop, basket, or a small table in the center of a circle. Students stand back approximately eight feet and see how many times they can "hop" their frog into the "pond" in a given time-frame.

| #7 | A to Z |
|---|---|

There are a number of activities that can be played using the letters of the alphabet. Three suggestions follow. Have the students come up with others.

**Number of players:** 6-20

**Equipment:** 26 Mini SpaceStations, stop watch, and a rope or lines on the floor to mark the alphabet area (about 15 feet x 30 feet)

**Preparation:** Write a different letter of the alphabet on each of 26 Mini SpaceStations. Randomly place the Mini SpaceStations in a rectangular area approximately 15 feet x 30 feet.

## The Alphabet Game

**Directions:** The students have two minutes to select a runner and develop a strategy. On the word "go," all students run to the alphabet area. The runner stands inside the letter area while all others must stay around the perimeter. The runner must touch each letter in alphabetical order with his/her toe, with only verbal help from the group. After the runner touches all the letters in proper sequence, everyone returns to the starting place as quickly as possible. Time them.

**Objective:** To have a selected member of the group touch each letter of the alphabet as quickly as possible, with verbal assistance from the rest of the group.

**Suggestion:** Give the group two minutes to develop a new strategy and try to do it again in less time.

## The Word Game

**Directions:** The students have two minutes to select a runner and develop a strategy. On the word "go," all students run to the alphabet area. The runner stands inside the alphabet area and all others must stay around the perimeter. As a group, the students cooperatively think up words, and the runner picks up each letter as teammates spell it. The students should use as many letters as possible. They get one point for each letter in the words they spell. Subtract the number of letters that remain from the total number of letters used to spell the words.

**Objective:** To use as many letters of the alphabet as possible in spelling words, using each letter only once.

**Suggestion:** Give the group two minutes to develop a new strategy to see if they can get a better score in another try.

## The Name Game

**Directions:** On the word "go," all students run to the alphabet area and take turns going inside and touching each letter of their full first name with their toe. The team members may verbally assist in finding the letters while standing around the perimeter of the area. When all members of the group have had a turn touching the letters of their name, everyone runs back to the starting spot. Time them.

**Objective:** To see how quickly each member of the group can touch the letter-tiles to spell his/her name.

**Suggestion:** Give the group about two minutes to develop a new strategy and then have them do it again.

## #8 SOS

**Number of players:** 12-20

**Equipment:** one 6-foot x 12-foot mat (the boat), two carpet squares (life rafts), one rope about 20 feet long, and two boundary cones

**Preparation:** Place the carpet squares and rope on the big mat in one area of the gym. Set up two boundary cones 30 feet away and 12 feet apart.

**Directions:** The entire crew is in the boat (on the large mat) when it hits a reef and is swamped. The boat must be flipped over to keep it from sinking. The two life rafts may be used by some of the crew. They may attach themselves to the boat with the rope. The water is shark-infested, so no one may jump into it. Once the boat is completely flipped over it must be tugged into safe waters by the life-raft crews and the crew of the big boat. The boundary cones mark the entrance to safe waters.

**Objective:** To figure out a way to work together to flip the boat and move it and the life rafts to safety without losing anyone in the shark-infested water.

## #9  The Rolling River Raft

**Number of players:** 10-30

**Equipment:** the Rolling River Raft, two oars (two 1-1/2-inch diameter dowels, 24 inches long with a rubber cap on one end), approximately 60 tennis balls, two boundary cones, and a stop watch

**Preparation:** The participants have two minutes to come up with a plan. They first need to decide who and how many people are to be on the raft. Next they need to plan how they will use the balls to make it possible for the raft to "float" to its destination beyond the boundary cones. This rafting adventure will be timed.

**Objective:** For the group to devise a plan, work cooperatively, and navigate the raft to the destination as quickly as possible.

**Suggestion:** If the group becomes frustrated due to lack of success, stop the activity. Facilitate a short debriefing session to initiate new ideas to make the activity work. Try it again.

## Levels of Difficulty:

**Level 1:** The group floats the raft down the river to its destination as quickly as possible. They share ideas and come up with a plan to make the return trip faster.

**Level 2:** Use boundary cones to show the width of the river. Since there are rapids in the river, no one is allowed in the water. Roll balls in front of the raft from the banks of the river. See how quickly the crew can navigate the raft down the river to its destination.

**Level 3:** Same as level 2, but the raft hits a whirlpool and must make a 360-degree turn at some point along the way.

**Level 4:** There is a lake (half of a volleyball court works well) and the raft must be negotiated from one side of the lake to the other. There are two rowers on the raft and one aid (called the DW or designated water walker) who may walk on the water. No one else is allowed in or on the water, but must assist in the negotiation of the raft from the edge of the lake. The DW must strategically place the balls thrown from the shore in such a way that the raft can be negotiated from one side of the lake to the other as quickly as possible.

**Level 5:** Same as level 4 except there are two rafts, one at either end of the lake. Each raft has its own DW. When the rafts meet in the middle of the lake the rowers exchange rafts. They must continue their trip on the new raft back to the side of the lake from which they began.

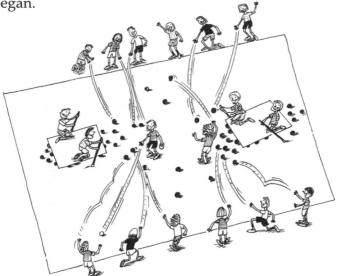

## #10          Frogs and Flies

**Number of players:** 10-30

**Equipment:** Enough tennis balls for half the group

**Preparation:** Divide the class into two equal groups. The frogs sit in a scattered formation with a tennis ball (the food) placed between their legs at least six inches away from all body parts.

**Directions:** On the word go the frogs close their eyes and try to protect their food from the flies. This is done by constantly moving their arms and hands over the food without actually touching it. Their eyes must remain closed at all times. The flies try to snatch the food without the frog knowing it. If a frog suspects the food is about to be stolen, he/she "squirts" (making a PSST noise). Each frog may "squirt" twice, once with each index finger. A fly that is "squirted" or touched by a frog's hand or arm is paralyzed. A paralyzed player sits and watches until the game is over. The game ends on the signal "stop". Thirty seconds is a good length of time for younger players. Older groups may play for one minute. Have the frogs and flies exchange roles and repeat the game.

**Objective:** Developing honesty, trust, fair play, responsible behavior, and fun. The frogs must not peek and the flies must accept being paralyzed. The flies must be patient, quick, and have good timing to succeed. The frogs must listen carefully for clues to know where the flies are. Both tasks are challenging!

Karl Rohnke taught this game to my students on one of his visits to the John Read Middle School. They loved it!

## #11 Floaters and Other Big-Ball Activities

**Number of players:** 20-30

**Equipment:** large SloMo Balls, Floaters, and Earth Balls (the older heavy "cage" balls are not recommended for these activities)

**Preparation:** Have one ball for approximately every 10 students.

### SloMo Balls

Give each group a SloMo Ball (or large beach ball). How many times can the group hit the ball into the air. The same student may not hit the ball two times in succession. If the ball hits the ground, start counting from one again.

**Options:**

- Designate a circular area (a hoop) for each team. All team members must have at least one foot in the designated area as they try to keep the ball in the air.
- Give each player a number. The ball must be hit by players in numerical order.

## Floaters

**Floater Juggling:** Each group has a Floater, which they attempt to keep in the air. Have the Floater come to rest on their hands before they send it floating back into the air. Do not punch or use force to keep the Floater up.

### Options:

- Have each group use the different-shaped Floaters—round, square, and triangular.
- Have one group hit a Floater into the air three times and then pass it to the second group. The second group hits it three times and then sends it on to the third group. Add a second Floater and then a third, and pass them from circle to circle.

**Floater Passing:** Have the class form a double line facing one another. Ask them to lie down, so that their feet touch the feet of the person across from them. Start the Floater at one end, and see if the students can successfully move it to the other end of the line by just using their feet. It may be timed and repeated after discussing ways to do it more quickly.

**Floater Chasing:** The class is divided into two circles, an outer circle and an inner circle, with students in the two circles facing each other. (The outer circle has more people.) With the two circles working together, the students practice moving a Floater around the circle, keeping it as close to the ground as possible. When the group can successfully keep the ball moving at a good rate of speed, choose one student to "chase" the ball until she or he catches up to it and touches it. That student then selects another person to chase the ball.

**Variation:** Have the square Floater chase the round Floater.

# #12 Alphabet Concentration Relay

**Number of players:** 20-30

**Equipment:** six numbered cones (1 through 6) and 156 tennis balls. Write a letter on each ball, making six complete alphabets. Write the letters of each alphabet set in a different color.

**Preparation:** Scatter the balls around the center of the room. Set the cones to make a large circle around the balls, as shown in the following figure.

**Directions:** Have an equal number of students line up behind each cone. The first person in each line runs to the center to find an A and places it next to his or her team's cone, then goes to the end of the line. The second person in each line finds a B, and so on until all teams have completed the alphabet.

**Options:**

1. Challenge the teams to find as many different letters as they can in a two-minute period.
2. Require the teams to find all the letters of the alphabet in the same color.
3. Ask the teams to make as many words as they can. The words must be formed in the order that the balls are retrieved.

# #13 Number Concentration Relay Activity

**Number of players:** 20-30

**Equipment:** cones numbered 1 through 8, 40 Mini SpaceStations, and 40 pieces of paper with eight sets of numbers (1 through 5)

**Preparation:** Scatter the Mini SpaceStations around the center of the room. Randomly place the numbered pieces of paper under the Mini SpaceStations. Set the eight cones in a large circle around the Mini SpaceStations.

**Directions:** Have an equal number of students line up behind each cone. On a signal to begin, the first person in each line runs to a Mini Space Station inside the circle. He or she picks it up and looks at the number on the paper that was hidden under the Mini SpaceStation. If the number on the paper is the same number as their team cone, it is brought back to the cone. If the number on the paper is not the same as his/her cone, the paper is placed back under the Mini SpaceStation, the student does three jumping jacks, then returns, going to the end of the line. The next person in each line repeats the task as soon as the previous teammate returns. If a student lifts a Mini SpaceStation and finds no paper (because another student matched the number to their cone number), he/she does three jumping jacks and returns empty handed. The activity continues until one team finds all five of the numbers that correspond to its cone number.

**Options:**

1. Use the same format as above. After completing the activity, give the teams one minute to form a strategy to do the activity more quickly. Repeat the activity.

2. Use the same format as above, but have a time limit of two minutes.

3. Use the same format as above, except place three wild cards under the Mini SpaceStations. A student who finds a wild card returns to his/her cone. A wild card gives the team two points, which are added to the numbered cards for the team's final score.

4. Use the same format as above, except each team tries to accumulate as few points as possible in a given amount of time.

5. Use any of the above activities, but have the students dribble a ball as they come and go.

Original idea from Don Puckett.

## #14        The 10K

**Number of players:** 10-100

**Equipment:** boundary cones

**Introduction:** Ask your students the following questions:

- How many miles is a 10K?
- What kind of physical training is necessary to run the 10K?
- About how long would it take to run the 10K for a 12-year-old? a high school track star? an Olympic runner?
- What kind of warm-up would you recommend to someone about to run the 10K?

**Directions:** Have the students pair up, with one being the runner and one being the coach. The coach directs the runner in a series of warm-up exercises and gives a brief "pep talk." As the race is about to begin, the coaches gather in the center of the gym or field, while each runner gets into a circle around them.

On the signal, the runners begin their race, and their coaches cheer them on.

After a three-minute run, the partners change places, and the event is repeated. When both partners have completed their run, they can compare their experiences and their feelings of accomplishment.

Appropriate music can help create the desired atmosphere for this special event.

**Objective:** This activity is a great icebreaker or closure activity. The goal is for each student to experience the roles of coach and competitor.

## #15 Round Ball

**Number of players:** 4-8 (two-on-two, three-on-three, four-on-four)

**Equipment:** one round ball goal, basketball, and Instant-Bounds boundary markers (vinyl lines 14 inches x 2-7/8 inches)

**Preparation:** Delineate a circle with a 20-foot radius. The circle begins from the basketball pole.

**Directions:** Organize the students into teams for two-on-two, three-on-three, or four-on-four. Play begins with one team bringing the ball in from outside the circle. The player must complete a pass before a shot can be taken. No dribbling is allowed.

If a shot is made from inside the circle, the team is awarded two points and possession of the ball. If a shot is made from outside the circle, the team is awarded three points and possession of the ball.

If a shot is missed, teammates can shoot again; but if the opponent rebounds the ball, the ball must be passed outside of the circle before a shot can be taken. All other basketball rules apply.

# 6th Inning

# Exercises With the Magic Rope

**Magic rope activities help students meet the following content standards:**

1. Demonstrates competency in many movement forms and proficiency in a few movement forms.
2. Applies movement concepts and principles to the learning and development of motor skills.
3. Exhibits a physically active lifestyle.
4. Achieves and maintains a health-enhancing level of physical fitness.

In the summer of 1961, I had the distinct privilege of taking a two-week movement education course. The teachers were Dr. L. Diem and Mrs. I. Nicole, two visiting professors from Germany. Dr. Diem authored the book *Who Can*. The two-week course completely changed my concepts and techniques of elementary physical education.

One idea that I gleaned from the class was how to facilitate all kinds of movement activities using the "magic rope." The magic rope is an elasticized rope, approximately 1/4-inch in diameter and 30 feet in length. The following examples explore the teaching of various activities from simple locomotor movements to the cartwheel and high jump. The teaching progressions make it easier for the students to grasp the basic skills necessary to learn the cartwheel and high jump. The "magic rope" also allows me to teach the concepts to the entire class at one time. The magic rope can be purchased from Things from Bell, P.O. Box 135, East Troy, WI 53120.

The advantages of using a stretch rope over a regular rope are as follows:

- If a student accidentally hits the rope, he/she is less likely to trip over it.
- The teacher can work with the entire class, varying the length of the rope as needed.
- The children are fascinated by its elasticity and enjoy using it to develop a variety of skills.

### Stretch rope activities done at a 90° angle

- Students run and jump over the rope with a one-foot take-off.

- Students crawl under the rope or two parallel ropes. The rope holders should keep the rope(s) low to the floor but high enough to make crawling under possible.

- Students squirm on their tummies like snakes under the rope or ropes.
- Students hop on one foot over the rope.
- Students skip over the rope.
- Students run and turn 180 degrees while going over the rope and then continue moving backward.
- Using two ropes laid flat on the ground, the students run and jump over the ropes, taking off on one foot and landing on two. One rope should be laid straight and the other at an angle, so the students can select the jumping distance that is comfortable for them.
- Students run over the rope as it is wiggled like a snake.
- Students run and "jump the brook" which is low at first and then jump again as the water rises.

### Window jumping

- Hold one rope about two to three feet above the other. Students run and step over the first rope while at the same time ducking to get under the second rope. One rope is above the other:
- Hold one rope about one foot off the floor. Hold a second rope about three feet behind the first and two to three feet higher. Students run and step over the first rope and duck under the second.

### Moving horizontally down the magic rope

Have students move over the rope from one side to the other. Vary the height of the rope according to the age and skill of the students. The students may skip, jump, or hop over the rope as they move from one end to the other.

**Progressive teaching of the cartwheel**

- Teach the students how to do a "supporting exercise" (balancing on hands, with hips over shoulders and knees tucked in)—some call it a donkey kick.

- With the rope on the ground, have the students form a line at one end of the rope. Have them slowly do the supporting exercise over the rope, with the hands going over the rope first and supporting the body as the legs are brought over. Students repeat the movement to the other side as they move down the rope.
- Raise the rope in small increments as the students' skill increases. Before you know it, they will be doing cartwheels!

### Using the magic rope to teach the high jump

- Students approach the rope at an angle and jump, taking off on the outside foot and leading with the inside foot. Students should jump from both sides to learn which side feels most natural. Once the preferred lead leg is established, allow them to jump from the side they prefer. Start with the rope low and gradually increase the height as the students' skill improves.

- Have two ropes, one higher than the other. Students may choose the rope they prefer.
- Have students jump one rope, and if they succeed, they move to one a little higher. If they miss, they remain (if they are at the lowest) or go to the next lowest.

# 7th Inning

# Line Dances

Students demonstrate the following content standards through line dancing:

1. Demonstrates competency in many movement forms and proficiency in a few movement forms.
2. Applies movement concepts and principles to the learning and development of motor skills.
3. Exhibits a physically active lifestyle.
7. Understands that physical activity provides opportunities for enjoyment, challenge, self-expression, and social interaction.

Line dancing is ideal for middle school students. They learn basic dance steps without a partner! Begin with the basic moves, and as the students become more proficient, gradually add more complex steps.

Demonstrate the dance moves with your back to the students, so they can mimic you. Teach one or two moves and practice them a few times. Teach another move and practice all of them from the beginning. Repeat until the students have practiced the whole dance, and then do it to music. If the dance has turns, select three students who know the dance and place one in each corner, so that other students can follow them as they turn.

**The teacher with his three helpers!**

Listed below are some of my favorite line dances.

# #1 "Love Me Like a Rock"

*Music: "Love Me Like a Rock," by Paul Simon*
Left, together, left—clap.
Right, together, right—clap.
Left, together, left—clap.
Right, together, right—clap.
Back 2-3-4. (Take four steps backward at half speed.)
Do a half circle forward.
Repeat from the beginning.

# #2 "Amos Moses"

*Music: "Amos Moses," by Gerry Reed*

Step with the right heel and back.

Step with the left heel and back.

Step forward with the right foot.

Drag the left foot behind the right.

Step forward again with the right foot and make a quarter turn to the right, sliding the left foot to the right.

Repeat from the beginning.

# #3 "The Three-Quarter-Hitch Line Dance"

*Music: "Love Shack," by the B 52's*

Two counts: Step to the right, bring left foot together.

Two counts: Step to the left, bring right foot together.

Four counts: Repeat.

Four counts: Circle the right finger in the air three times, clapping hands in air on the fourth beat.

Four counts: Circle the left finger in the air four times, clapping hands in air on the fourth beat.

Four counts: Grapevine to the right.

Four counts: Grapevine to the left.

Two counts: Slide diagonally forward to the right, bringing left together.

Two counts: Slide diagonally forward to the left, bringing right together.

Two counts: Slide diagonally back to the right, left together.

Two counts: Slide diagonally back to the left, right together.

Four counts: Jump three times, turning a quarter turn to the right each time. Clap on the fourth beat.

Four counts: Jump three times, turning to the left each time (returning to the original position). Clap on the fourth beat.

Repeat from the beginning.

Created by students Brett Ambler and John Santarella (a graduation gift to Mr. Hichwa) John Read Middle School, June, 1995

# #4 "Lion Sleeps Tonight"

*Music: "Lion Sleeps Tonight," by The Tokens*

Slide left foot forward.

Slide right foot forward with a quarter turn to the right.

Take three grapevine steps to the left (step left, right foot behind left, step left, clap).

Take three grapevine steps to the right (step right, left foot behind right, step right, clap).

Take three grapevine steps to the left (step left, right foot behind left, step left, clap).

Take three steps back with the right, left, right.

Repeat from the beginning.

# #5 "Louisiana Saturday Night"

*Music: "Louisiana Saturday Night," by Mel McDaniel, or "Twist and Shout," by Mary Chapin Carpenter*

Tap right foot (on toes) two times in front.

Run in place right, left, jump (slight pause), clap.

Tap left foot (on toes) two times in front.

Run in place left, right, jump (slight pause), clap.

Repeat once from the beginning.

Quick grapevine step to the right.

Hop two times on the right foot, two on the left, two on the right.

Then grapevine left, hop two times on the left foot, two on the right, two on the left.

Grapevine right, hop two times on the right foot, two on the left, two on the right.

Grapevine left, hop two times on the left foot, two on the right, two on the left.

Repeat from the beginning.

# #6 "The Wanderer"

*Music: "The Wanderer," by Dion; choreographed by Lee Gilman Scott and Joe Johnston*

Four counts: Tap right toe to the right side and back.

Repeat.

Four counts: Tap left toe to the left side and back.

Repeat.

Four counts: Tap right toe to the right side.

Touch right toe behind left foot.

Tap right toe to the right side.

Bring right toe up in front of left leg.

Four counts: Grapevine to the right with a quarter turn to the right on the fourth beat.

Four counts: Walk back with the left, then right, left, and a quick right and left in place.

Repeat from the beginning.

# #7 "Western Slide"

*Music: "If Bubba Can Dance, I Can Too," by Shenandoah*

Grapevine right three steps, kick, and clap.

Grapevine left three steps, kick, and clap.

Step back three steps, kick.

Step forward on left and stomp right.

Step backward on right and stomp left.

Step forward on left, scuff right foot forward, and do a quarter turn on the left foot.

Start again with a grapevine right.

# #8 "Superfreak"

*Music: "Get Outta My Car, Get Into My Life," by Billy Ocean*

Right hand palm down, point two times right.

Left hand palm down, point two times left.

Right hand palm up, point two times right.

Left hand palm up, point two times left.

Hitchhike right, two times.

Hitchhike left, two times.

Roll down two times (both hands).

Roll up two times (both hands).

Point down to the left with right hand twice.

Point down to the right with the left hand twice.

Slap left thigh with right hand.

Slap right thigh with left hand.

Right slap on right hip.

Left slap on left hip.

With both hands still on hips, jump forward two times.

On the third jump, cross feet.

On the fourth jump, uncross feet and make a quarter turn to the right.

# #9 "Here It Is"

*Music: "Gonna Make You Sweat: Everybody Dance Now," by C.C. and the Music Factory; choreographed by Gregg Montgomery*

Two arms point up to the right two times.

Two arms point up to the left two times.

Two arms point down the right two times.

Two arms point down to the left two times.

Two arms point up to the right one time.

Two arms point up to the left one time.

Two arms point down the right one time.

Two arms point down to the left one time.

Cross right arm to heart, as in the Pledge of Allegiance. (Hold.)

Cross left arm to right chest the same way. (Hold.)

Place right hand on right buttocks. (Hold.)

Place left hand on left buttocks. (Hold.)

Chug forward with a little jump. (Say "Ho.")

Chug forward with a quarter turn to the right. (Say "Ho.")

Repeat dance.

# #10 "Macarena"

*Music: "Macarena," by Los Del Mar (radio version)*

One count: Right hand in front, palm down.

One count: Left hand in front, palm down.

One count: Right hand in front, palm up.

One count: Left hand in front, palm up.

One count: Right hand across body, touch left shoulder.

One count: Left hand across body, touch right shoulder.

One count: Right hand to right ear.

One count: Left hand to left ear.

One count: Right hand to left thigh.

One count: Left hand to right thigh.

One count: Right hand to right hip.

One count: Left hand to left hip.

Four counts: Wiggle body forward, back, forward with a quarter turn to the right.

Repeat from the beginning.

# #11 "The Bunny Hop"

*Music: "All Shook Up," by Elvis Presley*

Right heel touch two times.

Left heel touch two times.

Jump forward once on two feet. (Hold one count.)

Jump back on two feet. (Hold one count.)

Hop three times forward on two feet.

Repeat.

# #12 "Continental"

*Music: "Kansas City," by Wilbert Harrison*

Four counts: Two steps to the right (step, together, step, together).

Four counts: Two steps to the left (step, together, step, together).

Four counts: Walk forward three steps (right, left, right). On the fourth count turn right a quarter turn as you swing left leg in front.

Four counts: Back up left, right, left, together.

Repeat from the beginning.

# #13 "Mountain Music"

*Music: "Mountain Music," by Alabama*

Four counts: Grapevine right.

Four counts: Grapevine left.

Four counts: Walk backward four steps.

Two counts: Walk forward with the right foot and bring the left together.

Two counts: Click heels two times with an enthusiastic "Yee-Haw."

Two counts: Tap right foot forward twice.

Two counts: Tap right foot back twice.

Three counts: Tap right foot forward once, backward once, and to the side once.

One count: Bring the right leg up and around the front, turning a quarter turn to the left.

Repeat from the beginning.

# #14 "Hully Gully"

*Music: "Baby Likes to Rock It," by The Tractors; choreographed by Don Puckett.*

Four counts: Grapevine to the right; finish with a hop on the right, kicking up with the left.

Four counts: Grapevine to the left; finish with a hop on the left, kicking up with the right.

Seven counts: Right hop forward, left hop forward, walk right, left, right.

One counts: Hop with a quarter turn to the right, kicking up with the left foot.

Four counts: Walk backward left, right, left, hopping on left, kicking up with right.

Repeat from the beginning.

# #15 "A Portuguese Line Dance"

*Music: "Quem, Quem, Quem" ("Who, Who, Who") by Onda Choc*

Two counts: Two hands up to the right two times.

Two counts: Two hands up to the left two times.

Two counts: Two hands down to the right two times.

Two counts: Two hands down to the left two times.

Four counts: Right hand twirl (left hand to right elbow) four times.

Four counts: Left hand twirl (right hand to left elbow) four times.

Four counts: Roll hands in front of you four times.

Four counts: Roll hands in opposite direction four times.

Four counts: Walk forward right, left, right—clap.

Four counts: Walk back left, right, left—clap.

Two counts: Jump forward. Hold one count.

Two counts: Jump backward. Hold one count.

Two counts: Jump a quarter turn right. Hold one count.

Two counts: Clap two times.

Repeat from the beginning.

# #16: "Cotton Eye Joe"

*Music: "Cotton Eye Joe," by Rednex, dance by Jerry Price*

Right toes tap down, right knee up, and shuffle to the right (1 and 2 and 3).

Left toes tap down , left knee up, and shuffle to the left (1 and 2 and 3).

Repeat.

Cha-cha right, cha-cha left, right pivot with a half turn left. Face back wall.

Cha-cha left, cha-cha right, left foot pivot with a quarter turn right. Face wall on right.

Cha-cha right, cha-cha left.

Repeat from the beginning.

# #17 "The Head-Tummy Dance"

*Music: Any music with a good beat; choreographed by students from Plymouth State College and the University of New Hampshire*

Form a circle with one person in the center. When the music starts, the student in the middle begins to dance to the beat of the music, and the remaining students follow the lead. After a few bars, the center dancer begins to rub his/her head a few times and then his/her tummy and finishes by making a lasso motion, moving toward someone in the outside circle. The lasso motion gives the signal for the chosen person to come in, and the dance repeats.

# 8th Inning

# Striking Skills
## Using a Paddle and a Volley Foam Ball

> **Being actively involved in striking skills will help students meet the following content standards:**
>
> 1. Demonstrates competency in many movement forms and proficiency in a few movement forms.
> 2. Applies movement concepts and principles to the learning and development of motor skills.
> 3. Exhibits a physically active lifestyle.
> 4. Achieves and maintains a health-enhancing level of physical fitness.
> 5. Demonstrates responsible personal and social behavior in physical activity settings.
> 7. Understands that physical activity provides opportunities for enjoyment, challenge, self-expression, and social interaction.

The closer the striking area of an implement is to the hand, the easier it is to hit a ball with it. Therefore, students should begin learning to strike a ball correctly using a paddle. Once they have become proficient with a paddle, they are more likely to find success with racket sports.

## #1   Grips and Warm-Up Drills

(directions for right-handed players)

**Equipment:** molded Pick-A-Paddle and uncoated Volley foam balls (90mm)

## Grips

**Forehand grip.** Hold the paddle with the left hand and shake hands with it with the right, extending the index finger in a trigger fashion.

**Backhand grip.** Turn the forehand grip a quarter turn counter-clockwise until the knuckle of the pointer finger is on top.

**Service and volley grip (the continental grip).** Hold the racket halfway between the forehand and backhand grips. Practice this grip by bouncing the ball on the floor with the edge of your paddle.

## Warm-Up Drills

1. **Forehand, ball on floor.** With a forehand grip, bounce the ball on the floor at least 10 times no higher than your waist.
2. **Forehand, ball in air.** With a forehand grip, bounce the ball up into the air at least 10 times about head high.

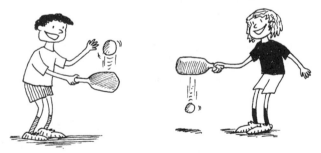

3. **Backhand, ball in air.** With a backhand grip, bounce the ball into the air at least 10 times.
4. **Continental, ball in air.** Using the continental grip, bounce the ball into the air 10 times, hitting one side of the paddle and then the other.

## Check Points

- **Forehand grip.** Do you see a V between the index finger and thumb?
- **Backhand grip.** Is the knuckle of the pointer finger on top?
- **Service and volley grip.** Can you bounce the ball on the ground with the edge of the paddle?

## #2       Forehand Volley

(directions for right-handed players)

1. **Practice throwing.** Face your partner and step forward with your left foot as you throw the ball underhand to a partner. Your partner throws the ball back in a like manner. Make 10 throws each.

2. **Throwing and catching.** Throw the ball underhand at your partner's right shoulder. Your partner, facing you, catches it with his/her hand held in the position of a police officer stopping traffic. Throw and catch 10 turns each.

3. **Ready position.** Face your partner with your knees comfortably bent. Use the continental grip and hold the paddle in front of you, cradled at the throat with your other hand.

4. **Practice volleying.** Throw the ball underhand to your partner's right shoulder. Your partner, in a ready position, holds a paddle using a continental grip and volleys (punches) the ball back. Take 10 turns each.

## Check Points

- Are you facing the net?
- Are you stepping forward with your left foot?
- Does the punch motion begin at the shoulder?

| #3 | Backhand Volley |
|---|---|

(directions for a right-handed player)

1. **Ready position.** Face your partner squarely, with your knees comfortably bent. Use the continental grip and hold the paddle in front of you, cradled at the throat with the other hand.

2. **Practice volleying.** Face your partner and hold the paddle by your left shoulder, placing your left hand behind the paddle. The thrower tosses the ball at the paddle. Hit the ball as you take a step forward with your right foot. Take 10 turns each.

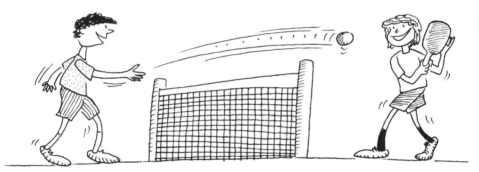

## Check Points

- Is your body facing the net?
- Are you stepping forward with your right foot?
- Does the punch motion begin at the shoulder?

## #4 Volleying Drills

1. **Continental grip.** Hold your paddle and bounce the ball on the floor with the edge of your paddle.

2. **Forehand volleys.** Both partners stand at their own service line (about 20 feet apart). Hit 10 forehand volleys back and forth to one another.

3. **Forehand to backhand.** Hit a forehand volley to your partner's backhand. Your partner returns the volley to your forehand. Repeat 10 times.

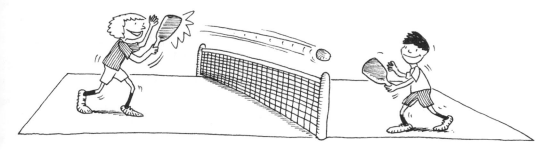

4. **Backhand to forehand.** Hit a backhand volley to your partner's forehand. Your partner returns the volley to your backhand. Repeat 10 times.

5. **Backhand to backhand.** Partners hit 10 backhand volleys to one another.

6. **Volleying.** How many consecutive volleys can you and your partner make?

| #5 | **Forehand** |
|---|---|

(directions for right-handed players)

1. **Drop and catch.** Stand with the left side facing the net or wall. With the right hand held back at the 6 o'clock position, drop the ball in front of your left foot. Catch the ball with your right hand while transferring your weight forward, finishing with your hand in the 12 o'clock position. Repeat 10 times.

2. **Partners drop and hit with hand.** Hold your right hand at the 6 o'clock position. Drop the ball in front of your left foot with your left hand. Hit the ball with your right hand, keeping your wrist firm and transferring your weight forward. Swing from low (just below the waist) to high (shoulder height) and hold the hand at the 12 o'clock position for 3 seconds. The partner, about 20 feet away, catches the ball and strokes it back in a similar manner. Repeat 10 times.

3. **Partners drop and hit with paddle.** Hold the paddle at the 6 o'clock position. Your partner, about 20 feet away, throws the ball so that you can hit it on the bounce. Gently stroke the ball back. Take 10 turns each.

4. **Drop and hit against the wall.** Stand with your left side facing the wall. Take the paddle back to the 6 o'clock position. Drop the ball in front of your left foot and stroke the ball toward a target on the wall three feet above the floor. Finish with the paddle facing the target. Catch the ball after it hits the wall and bounces off the floor. Repeat the exercise 10 times.

5. **Ready position and hit.** Face the net with your knees comfortably bent and your paddle held in front of you. With the ball in your left hand, turn to your right and drop it in front of your left foot. Hit the ball at the target on the wall. Return to the ready position after each hit. See how many times you can hit the ball without missing. What is your best score?

## Check Points

- Is your wrist firm as you make contact with the ball?
- Where is your paddle head at the end of the swing? Does it point to where you want the ball to go?
- Do you return to the ready position after each hit?

| #6 | **Backhand** |
|----|-----------|

(directions for right-handed players)

1. **Ready position.** Face the net with your knees comfortably bent. Hold the paddle in front of you, cradled at the throat with the left hand.

2. **Drop and hit.** Stand with your right side facing the net. Take the paddle back to the 6 o'clock position, placing your thumb to your left thigh. Step forward as you drop the ball next to your front foot and stroke through the ball toward the target, ending in the 12 o'clock position. Catch the ball after it bounces. Repeat 10 times.

3. **How many hits?** Repeat #2, but after the ball hits the wall and bounces off the floor, continue to stroke the ball as many times as possible, getting into the ready position after each stroke.

## Check Points

- Does your paddle start back at the thigh when you begin the stroke?
- Are you swinging from the shoulder?
- Is your racket at the 12 o'clock position at the end of the stroke?

## #7 The Serve

(directions for right-handed players)

1. **Grip.** Hold the racket with a continental grip. Bounce the ball on the floor with the edge of your racket a few times to check it!

2. **Throwing and catching with a partner.** Stand with your left side facing your partner, who is 20 feet away. Throw a ball overhand to your partner, transferring your weight forward onto your left foot. Make at least 10 throws each.

3. **Serve from back-scratch position.** Stand with your nondominant side facing a wall and your paddle in the back-scratch position. Position feet shoulder-width apart. Toss the ball, hit it at 1 o'clock toward the target, and follow through to opposite side, holding it for three seconds. How many times can you hit the target out of 10 tries?

4. **Serve with full swing.** Swing your paddle back as you toss the ball in the air and hit it with the paddle at the target. How many times can you hit the target out of 10 tries?

## Check Points

- When you stroke the ball, does it feel as if you are throwing the paddle over the net?
- Is your arm fully extended when you hit the ball?
- Does your weight transfer forward onto your left foot as you swing through?
- Does your paddle end up on the left side of your body at the end of your swing?

## #8  The Short Tennis Game

Use half of the service area of a tennis court (or a smaller area). Drop the ball and hit it to your partner over a net (or net substitute, about three feet high). Your partner lets the ball bounce and hits it

back to you. See how many times you and your partner can hit the ball back and forth while keeping it within the boundary lines. What is your best score?

## #9  Bucket Drill

(If no court or net is available)

Place two buckets about 8 to 10 feet apart. Each player stands behind a bucket. Bounce the ball in front of you and try to hit it into the bucket at the other end. Your partner lets the ball bounce and strokes it back, trying to get it into your bucket. Work as a team and see how many times you and your partner can get the ball into a bucket. Try the same drill using the backhand stroke.

## #10        Partner Wall Drill

Stand about 20 feet from a wall. Drop the ball in front of you and hit it against the wall. Your partner lets the ball bounce and then strokes it against the wall. Take turns stroking the ball and see how many times you and your partner can hit the ball against the wall without missing. What is your best score? Try to hit a two foot x three foot target on the wall three feet from the floor. See how many times you and your partner can hit the target without missing. What is your best score? Try the same drill using the backhand stroke.

## #11      Four-Person Wall Drill

Four people stand about 20 feet from a wall, with one person behind the other. The first person bounces the ball, strokes it against the wall, and then moves quickly to the end of the line. The second person lets the ball bounce, then strokes it against the wall, and quickly moves to the end of the line. Continue with each player taking turns letting the ball bounce, stroking it against the wall, and then quickly moving to the end of the line. As a team, see how many strokes you can make in a row. What is your best score? Try the same drill using the backhand stroke.

## #12 The Lob Drill

(with partners)

One partner throws the ball and the other stands in the ready position. After the ball bounces, attempt to hit the ball over the head of the thrower. The striker contacts the ball with an open face, following through to the 12 o'clock position. Hit 10 lobs with the forehand and 10 with the backhand and switch positions.

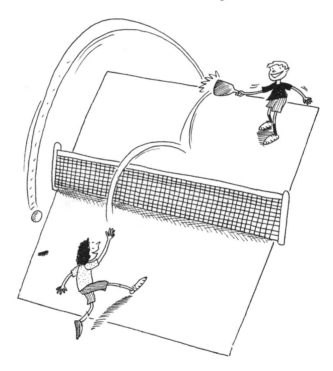

## Check Points

- Do you begin in the ready position?
- Does your paddle begin at the 6 o'clock and end at the 12 o'clock positions?
- Is the lob landing deep, near the baseline?

| #13 | **The Overhead** |
|---|---|

(with partners)

Have your partner hit a lob to you. Standing sideways at the net, position your racket as if you were to throw it over the net. As the ball approaches, point at it with your nonracket hand. Hit the ball, transferring your weight forward and follow through down to the opposite side of your body. Hit 10 overheads and switch.

## Check Points

- Did you point at the ball with your left hand while standing with your left side to the net?
- Did you start with your paddle in an overhand throwing position?
- Did your stroke end with the paddle on the left side of your body?

# 9th Inning

# International Games
## Understanding Cultural Diversity Through Sports

**Learning about and participating in international games help students meet the following content standards:**

1. Demonstrates competency in many movement forms and proficiency in a few movement forms.
2. Applies movement concepts and principles to the learning and development of motor skills.
3. Exhibits a physically active lifestyle.
4. Achieves and maintains a health-enhancing level of physical fitness.
5. Demonstrates responsible personal and social behavior in physical-activity settings.
6. Demonstrates understanding and respect for differences among people in physical-activity settings.
7. Understands that physical activity provides opportunities for enjoyment, challenge, self-expression, and social interaction.

In today's technological world, it is surprising that children are exposed to so few games of other cultures. By playing traditional games from other countries, children are introduced to new terminology, rules, and equipment. We hope it will also give them a better understanding of and appreciation for their counterparts around the world.

Many school systems today encourage interdisciplinary curriculum planning. A unit of international games in physical education could be planned around a geography unit and/or English unit about different parts of the world and different cultures. It could culminate with an International Games Field Day.

When introducing games from other countries, you should not require strict adherence to the rules anymore than you would when introducing traditional American games. Modifying the rules initially can be useful in developing the skills required, and making the teams small will increase participation.

Keep-away is a good warm-up activity for team handball and school rugby. See Game #2, 3rd Inning for details on how to introduce the keep-away concepts.

# Team Handball

(Denmark)

**Number of players:** two teams of four to six

**Equipment:** a team handball or any ball approximately 6 inches in diameter and two goals: field hockey goals, cones about 8 feet apart, or 6 foot x 12 foot mats hung on the walls.

**Playing area:** a gymnasium or outdoor play area about 50 feet x 100 feet. A semicircular crease drawn approximately 20 feet in front of the goals.

**Modified rules:** Players pass the ball to team members until someone is clear to shoot for a goal. The ball must be thrown from outside the crease. Players may dribble three times or take three steps with the ball. They may not hold the ball for more than three seconds before they pass, dribble, or shoot (penalty free throw). A penalty shot is taken 22 feet from the goal. Anytime a goal is scored, the goalie throws the ball back in play.

**Objective:** To score by throwing the ball into your opponents' goal and prevent the opponents from scoring.

**Scoring:** A point is scored when a ball is thrown from behind the crease and goes through the goal area. If cones are used as goals, the ball must hit the ground before it goes through them.

# School Rugby

(Great Britain)

**Number of players:** two teams of four to six

**Equipment:** a rugby ball or a football

**Playing area:** outside playing field with the end lines as goal lines

**Modified rules:** Play begins with a scrum. The referee rolls the ball between two lines of opposing players, who attempt to roll the ball backward with their feet. Whoever picks up the ball after it is kicked backward may run with it or pass it laterally or backward to a teammate in an attempt to move it toward the goal line.

If a player running with the ball is tagged (touched) by an opponent, the carrier must stop immediately and perform a "roll ball." A *roll ball* is the art of placing the ball on the ground and rolling it back with the foot. When a touch occurs, all defending players must stand five meters from the roll ball and cannot move in a forward direction until someone from the offensive team touches the ball. All offensive players must be situated behind the ball.

When a pass is not completed, the ball goes to the opposing team. This prevents players from competing for a fumble. All players must be stationed on their respective sides, that is, the defenders five meters behind the ball and the offensive players on their side of the ball. At this time, a roll ball occurs and play continues.

**Objective:** To score by running with the ball over the goal line.

**Scoring:** One point is scored when the ball is carried over the goal line.

**Variations:** One team is allowed six touches. If no score is achieved, then a change of possession occurs.

**Skill Drills:**

- Position four people in a line, approximately three feet apart from each other. Start passing the ball underhand to each other and back again.

- Do the skill drill above, except increase the distance between players. It can be made competitive if several lines begin at once. The object is to see which line can complete two rotations.

- In this drill, player A passes the ball laterally to player B and then runs to the end of the line as shown in the following diagram. This pattern continues with the last player beginning the scenario over again by passing the ball to player A. Once each player has received the ball twice, the ball is passed in the opposite direction until each player has again received it twice. This drill can be made competitive by having several lines passing the ball at the same time. The first team to complete the drill celebrates by giving each other a high-five.

- As the players run side-by-side down the field, Player A passes the ball laterally to Player B. Player B passes it to Player C, and so on to the last player. The ball is then passed in the opposite direction until the group has traveled to a designated point, approximately 30 yards down the field. Play continues as the team returns to its starting point.

References: P. Mathesins and B. Strand, *JOPERD* (April 1994)."Touch rugby: An alternative activity in physical education."

# Malha

(Portugal)

**Number of players:** two or four, playing individually or as teams

**Equipment:** one game disk for two players or two game disks for four players (Malha), two cylinders of wood (about 10 inches tall and 2 inches in diameter), and 20 Instant-Bounds.

**Playing area:** a gymnasium or outdoor play area

**Preparation:** Place the wooden cylinder in the center of a rectangular box made of 10 Instant-Bounds and another cylinder in a similar box about 34 feet away.

**Modified rules for four players:** The first player on the team stands behind the opponent's box and throws the Malha at the wooden cylinder in the box at the opposite end. If the cylinder is knocked down, it is replaced before the second person on the team throws the Malha at the target. Now the opponents take turns throwing the Malha at their target from their respective ends. The teams continue taking turns.

**Objective:** To knock down the cylinder of wood and keep the Malha inside the box.

**Scoring:** Three points are scored if the cylinder is knocked down and the Malha stays inside the box. Two points are scored if the cylinder is knocked down but the Malha lands outside the box. One point is scored if the Malha lands inside the box but does not knock the cylinder down. The person or team with the most points wins.

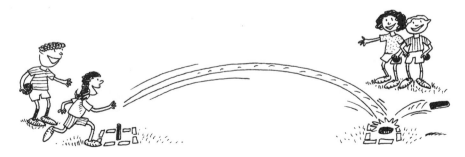

## Bocce

(Italian)

**Number of players:** four to eight. Each player may compete individually, or those with the same-colored disk may constitute a team.

**Equipment:** one Game Disk set (two each of four different colors, plus a pink disk or marker)

**Playing area:** a gymnasium or outdoor play area

**Modified rules:** The first player tosses the "spike" or sometimes called the "jack" (pink disk) 15 feet to 30 feet away. Each successive player takes a turn tossing his or her disk as close to the marker as possible, starting from where the marker was thrown. The player who tossed the marker throws last. The player whose disk lands closest to the marker scores one point and gets to toss the marker for the next game.

**Objective:** To score by getting your game disk closest to the marker.

**Scoring:** The player or team whose disk lands closest to the pink disk scores one point.

# Rounders

(Great Britain)

**Number of players:** two teams of six to nine

**Equipment:** four 1-1/2-foot-long sticks (bats), a ball about the size of a Little League baseball, four posts (bases) three feet three inches tall, held upright by a heavy base

**Playing area:** a gymnasium or outdoor play area

**Modified rules:** Rounders is somewhat similar to baseball. A batter tries to hit a pitched ball and run to touch the four posts to score a "rounder" (run). Fielders have no set positions, and there are no foul balls. All hit balls are good. All team members bat once before the teams exchange places. Players must remain in the same batting order each inning they are up.

**Bowling (pitching):** The bowler must throw the ball underhand between the batter's head and knees and inside the batting square to be valid. A pitch that does not meet these criteria is called a no-ball. The batter remains at bat until a successful hit is made.

**Running the track (bases):** When a ball is hit, the batter runs to the first post or continues on to the other posts. If the runner chooses to stop at a post, the runner must maintain contact with the post to be safe. One runner may not pass another runner or remain at the same post as another. A runner may try to steal a base.

**Outs:** A batter is out if touched by a fielder with the ball before reaching a post, if a fielder in possession of the ball touches a post that a runner is forced to run to, if a runner passes another runner, or if a runner runs on the inside of a post. There is no limit to the number of outs a team may make.

**Scoring:** A rounder (run) is scored only if the batter hits a ball and successfully runs outside the first three posts and to the fourth, touching each post as she or he goes. The team with the most rounders wins. Any team member at a post continues around when a ball is hit, but that person's completion doesn't count as a rounder. Only a home run can count as a rounder.

## Ming, Mang, Mung

(Korea)

**Number of players:** 8 to 30

**Equipment:** none

**Playing area:** just a comfortable place to sit in a circle

**Rules:** The class sits in circle. A player is designated to begin the game by saying "ming" and simultaneously pointing to anyone in the circle. The point should be vigorous, with the student saying "ming" and making eye contact with the person at whom she or he is pointing. The person directly to the pointer's right says "mang" and points to anyone in the circle. The point should be decisive.

The person sitting to the right of that pointer similarly points to someone in the circle and says "mung." The person who is the receiver of the point says "ming," and the sequence continues.

If someone makes a mistake by pointing or speaking out of turn or too slowly, all participants put their thumbs in the circle. The group says with emotion and conviction, "You're out!" and brings their thumbs back over their shoulders. Since all elimination games have been outlawed in our class, the individual who made an egregious error excuses himself or herself from the game circle and takes on another role outside the circle as the designated heckler (DH). The role of the DH is to try to coax those people left in the game to make a mistake and have them join the DH circle. The DH is not allowed to physically touch a player or in any way block a player's view. The game continues until there are four players left—the final four.

This game was taught to me by Ann Yang, one of my sixth grade class members, who learned it in her native Korea.

# Cricket

(Great Britain)

**Number of players:** two teams of 6 to 11

**Equipment:** two cricket bats, a ball (a rubber ball for outside or a Wiffle ball about four inches in diameter for inside), two wickets (three 28-inch vertical stumps set into a nine-inch-wide base), and a bail (a stick about nine inches long and one and one-half inches in diameter that rests across the wicket stumps)

**Playing area:** a gymnasium or playing field with the wickets set 30 feet to 40 feet apart

**Modified rules:** American baseball was developed from cricket. In both games, one player bowls (pitches) a ball and an opposing player tries to hit the ball with a bat and score runs. The team scoring the most runs wins.

### The Bowler (pitcher):

- The bowler stands behind the crease and throws the ball underhand or over-hand with a straight arm (arm swings up past the ear). The bowler tries to knock the bail off the wicket while, at the same time, preventing the batsman from making a good hit. The bowler may not step over the crease while bowling but may bounce the ball on the ground in front of the batsman.

- After facing six batsmen, a new bowler takes his/her place. Each time there is a new bowler, the balls are thrown toward the other wicket.

**The Batsman:**

- The batsman stands in front of the crease with the bat down by his/her feet. The batsman attempts to make a good hit while also preventing the bail from being knocked off the wicket.
- The batsman must carry the bat with him/her while running to a wicket. If it is dropped, the batsman must pick it up before continuing.
- The runners need only touch their bats over the crease to be safe or to score a run.
- Each time the batsman and the second batter at the other wicket successfully exchange places, a run is scored. These batsmen continue to hit and exchange places until they are put out.
- There are no foul balls. All hits are good.
- The teams exchange places when all members of the batting team have made an out.
- When a ball is hit and caught on the fly by a fielder, the batter is out, but the other runner may advance if she or he had passed the batsman before the ball was caught. If the runner had not passed the batsman before the ball was caught, the runner returns to the wicket where he or she started, and a new batsman is up.
- There are no double plays in cricket.

**Outs:**

A batsman is out

- if the bowler knocks the bail off the wicket,
- a hit ball is caught on the fly, or
- a fielder holding the ball in his/her hand knocks the bail off the wicket with the ball before the batsman reaches the wicket.

# Sepak Takraw

(Thailand, Malaysia, Burma, Laos, India, and the Philippines)

**Number of players:** three to five. Officially, there are three players to a team.

**Equipment:** a Buka Ball

**Playing area:** The game is played on an official badminton court.

**Lead-up games:**
1. Each player attempts to keep the Buka Ball in the air using any part of the body except the hands and arms.
2. A group of players (three or more) attempt to keep the Buka Ball off the ground for as long as possible.

**The net game:** Sepak Takraw is played by two teams of three or four players over a five-foot net. The buka can be hit up to three times before it must cross the net. Any player may hit the ball three times in succession.

**Objective:** To hit the buka over the net without the opponents being able to return it.

**Scoring:** The serving team scores a point by hitting the buka over the net and having the opposing team unable to return it. Only the serving team can score points—15 points = one game. A set is winning two out of three games.

**Faults:**

- A player does not kick the buka over the net on a serve.
- The buka falls to the ground inside or outside of the court.
- The buka is hit more than three times on one side of the court.
- The buka hits the net during the game on a serve and it doesn't go over.
- A player allows the ball to hit his/her arm or hand.
- A player allows any body part to touch or go over the net.
- A player commits a held ball.

**Strategies:** Similar to volleyball. Each team attempts to control the buka, setting it up and then spiking it into the opposing court.

**Basic individual skills:** The inside-foot kick, the outside-foot kick, the front-foot kick, and the thigh kick.

## Lacrosse

**Number of players:** 3 to 6 players per team—small teams are preferred for the less experienced players

**Equipment:** one lacrosse stick and a ball for each student, scrimmage vests, dome markers or Flow-Markers (four for every two teams if using grids), cones for goals (if goals are to be used)

**Playing area:** a gymnasium or playing field

**Basic skills:**

- Raking the ball from the ground and into the basket while stationary
- Raking the ball from the ground and into the basket while moving
- Jogging, running, and sprinting with the ball cradled in the basket without having it fall out.
- Tossing the ball underhand with the stick 8-10 inches above your head and catching it in the basket. Practice both right and left handed.
- Using the stick, make an overhead throw to your partner who catches it in his/her basket to throw the ball overhand to a partner.
    a. Stationary passer to stationary receiver
    b. Stationary passer to moving receiver
    c. Moving passer to stationary receiver
    d. Moving passer to moving receiver

The basic skills may be practiced in a large field or in "grids," either inside or outside.

### Modified game for practicing lacrosse skills:

**3 on 3.** Use a "grid" (approximately 30 feet x 30 feet) and no goals. Each team tries to make five consecutive catches. If the team is successful, the ball goes to the opponents who try to make five completions. Any time a pass is incomplete, the ball goes to the opposing team.

The following games are played in a grid. The size of the grid depends on how many students are on a team. Teams of three use a 50-foot x 100-foot grid. Teams of six use a 75-foot x 100-foot grid.

## Modified games

- 3 on 3—All players are roving players
- 4 on 4—Play with one offensive, one defensive, and two roving players on each team
- 5 on 5—Play with two offensive, two defensive, and one roving player on each team
- 6 on 6—Play with two offensive, two defensive, and two roving players on each team

Rovers are players who can play the entire field. Offensive players are limited to playing on the offensive side of the field. Defensive players are limited to playing on the defensive side of the field. They also protect the goal area, if one is used.

**Basic rules:**

- The ball must be passed over the midline of the field to a partner.
- No physical contact is allowed. Contact can only be made with the basket.

**Scoring:** A point can be scored using one of the two following methods: a completed pass to a partner who receives it over the goal line or a ball thrown into the opponent's goal. (If cones are used to designate the goal, the ball must hit the ground before it goes through the cones.)

**Objective:** To score more points than the opponent.

Reprinted from *MASSPEC Program Session Handouts Booklet: AAHPERD National Convention, 1997,* (1997) with permission from the National Association for Sport and Physical Education (NASPE), 1900 Association Drive, Reston, VA 20191-1599.

# Extra Innings

# Resources for Information

Familiarize yourself with Moving Into the Future—National Standards for Physical Education, A Guide to Content and Assessment. It can be purchased from

The National Association for Sport and Physical Education (NASPE)
1900 Association Drive
Reston, Virginia 22091
Phone: (800) 321-0789

Adventure programming was an essential ingredient in the educational offerings in my middle school. The indoor and outdoor ropes courses, rock climbing, new games, and various initiatives were very popular activities that the students could relate to and succeed in. For more information on the Project Adventure program, write or call

Project Adventure
P.O. Box 100
Hamilton, MA 01936
(508) 524-4556

# Additional Acknowledgments

I would like to acknowledge the following physical education teachers for their contributions:

---

Charles "Chip" Candy, 1995 NASPE National Middle School Teacher of the Year, for the upper-arm-strength activities, line dances, and his willingness to share activities.

Dr. Stevie Chepko and Dr. Lynn Couturier, professors at Springfield College, Springfield, Massachusetts, for the ideas in the "grid" games.

Ken Demas, middle school teacher in Mamaraneck, NY, for his willingness to share adventure concepts and games.

Barbara Morrill of Manchester, NH, for her idea of putting a beanbag frog on top of a playground ball.

Don Puckett of Winston Salem, NC, for his enthusiasm and encouragement in addition to his creative ideas.

Jim Ross and Gregg Montgomery for their sharing of line dances and their support and encouragement at Camp Caesar and at the New Jersey Lake Conference.

John Smith, 1989 NAPSE National Elementary Teacher of the Year, for all his help and expertise, especially for his Dyna-Bands routine and the Jump Flags.

---

# Equipment

The following equipment mentioned in this book can be purchased from Sportime International, One Sportime Way, Atlanta, GA 30340, (800) 444-5700.

All-Balls (6-inch)™
BB-Trainers™
Beanbag frogs™
Big Blue volleyballs™
Buka Balls
CatchBalls™
Dome MultiMarkers™
Dyna-Bands
FB-Trainer™
Float-R™
Flow-Markers™
Frisbees
Fan Balls
Game Disks™
Hands-on basketballs™
Instant-Bounds™
Jump Flags™
Junior team handballs
Kontrol-Kones™
Kwik Cricket

Learning Obstacle Boards™
Mini SpaceStations™
Molded Pick-A-Paddles
Nuclear Waste Transfer™
Playground balls
Rolling River Raft™
Rounders
Rubber chickens
Rugby balls
Shoulder Folders™
SloMo Balls™ (large and small)
Soccer balls
Spider Balls
Step-N-Stones™
Uncoated Volley Foam Balls (90mm)
Volleyball Gradeballs™

# About the Author

John Hichwa taught physical education in grades K-8 for 35 years. In his words, "The gymnasium and the playing field were my laboratory. It was there that I had the opportunity to try out new ideas, make a difference in the lives of my students, and form my vision of how physical education can play an important role in the lives of all students."

Now an education consultant, Hichwa continues to influence the field of physical education. In the summer of 1997, he taught physical education activities to young Japanese children at the American School in Japan Summer Day Camp, located just outside of Tokyo. And he is still a popular featured presenter at conferences, conventions, and workshops across the country.

Hichwa has received numerous awards over the course of his career, including 1993 Middle School Physical Education Teacher of the Year, presented by the National Association for Sport and Physical Education, and the 1997 CAHPERD Honor Award, presented by the Connecticut Association for Health, Physical Education, Recreation and Dance. In 1981 he started a Project Adventure program at the John Read Middle School in West Redding, CT. The program, which became an integral part of the school curriculum as well as Project Adventure's model for middle school adventure programs, was featured on national television in 1987.

Hichwa lives in Redding, CT, with his wife Marion. They enjoy tennis, bicycling, and traveling.

# About the Illustrator

Pedro Leitão is a professional illustrator and cartoonist. He is a regular illustrator for the Portuguese versions of *Sesame Street Magazine* and *Elle* and a cartoonist for *IPAMB*, a monthly educational newsletter for the Portuguese Institute for Environmental Awareness. He illustrated *O Casamento da Gata* (The Kitten's Wedding), a 24-page, full-color children's book authored in verse by a well-known Portuguese writer of children's literature. A highlight of his career was working as an artist in residence at the Stivers Middle School of the Arts in Dayton, OH, from February 1991 through June 1992. Leitão is also a children's theater actor and scenographer. Born in Angola and a resident of Portugal, he holds a Licenciatura degree in painting from the Fine Arts School of Lisbon.